THE
JAPANESE
MANAGEMENT
MYSTIQUE

The Reality
Behind the Myth

JON
WORONOFF

PROBUS PUBLISHING COMPANY
Chicago, Illinois
Cambridge, England

Table of Contents

iii

Table of Contents

Preface

There are dozens, if not hundreds, of books by foreigners on Japanese management. They cover just about every aspect of that much discussed system. They look into all sorts of details and come up with any number of wondrous lessons that can be learned. But there is one thing they do not do, in the overwhelming majority of cases: they do not bother showing the system's weaknesses and failings.

That is the purpose of this book. It is perhaps not a very noble mission, but it is certainly an essential one. It is only by knowing the good *and* bad points, the strengths *and* weaknesses, the achievements *and* failures, that outsiders can understand Japanese-style management. Just looking at one side and ignoring the other is hardly a contribution to improved perception or increased comprehension.

Showing the other side of Japanese management has multiple merits for the practicing businessman, as opposed to the academic or student of things Japanese. It removes some of the aura of invincibility of Japanese companies, it knocks Japanese managers down a few pegs. That would be dangerous if foreign businessmen already underestimated them and would thereby be weakened. Alas, at present, the contrary impression prevails and too many foreigners assume they cannot fight back when, in fact, they can.

How can the competitive edge of foreign companies be sharpened? One view expressed by many overzealous teachers is to "learn from Japan." I agree wholeheartedly. But I do not feel that you can learn very much from the lessons presently suggested because, like the books, they only show Japan's strengths. There are also weaknesses. And it would be terribly risky to adopt some Japanese technique only to discover that it was not really that effective or simply could not work in another country or culture.

Learning lessons, however, will only help even out the situation. You will be able to do more things like the Japanese and, hopefully, as well as the Japanese, although that is doubtful. Indeed, the very idea of out-Japanesing the Japanese which is inherent in the "learn from Japan" ethos is a bit quixotic. Foreigners will at best be pale imitations and, if they fight the Japanese on Japanese terms, they will almost inevitably lose.

No, salvation must be sought in a different direction. Foreign companies and managers must be able to do something better than the Japanese. And that is where the description of Japan's weaknesses comes in. On the one hand, by knowing their weaknesses, you can determine your relative strengths and use them more effectively. On the other, by knowing their weaknesses, you can take advantage of them. You can exploit Japanese failings to overcome your Japanese rivals.

I apologize for sounding like a *judo* master at this point, but I sincerely believe that the only hope for foreign businessmen is to study the Japanese more carefully, establish a more exact inventory of their weak points and, in short, know your foe. Then you can use your strengths in combination with their weaknesses to prevail.

Better a *judo* master than an ivory tower academic. As with all my books, this one is intended to be of practical use and is therefore written in simple, straightforward language. Theory is left aside, especially when it is erroneous theory that has little basis in hard facts. And I have better things to do than align myself with the existing academic schools of Japanese management. On the other hand, I do refer to what the Japanese themselves think of Japanese management and which is often not as flattering as the prevailing foreign views.

So, read on. It is about time some of the familiar myths and illusions of Japanese superiority in management were dissipated. Their loss will be your gain. The closer you come to reality, a more mixed and less admirable reality than you had been led to expect, the easier it will be to cooperate with or compete against the Japanese.

Jon Woronoff

1

The Japanese Management Boom

Foreign Myth Making

■ Few intellectual movements have proliferated with the speed and vigor of the Japanese management boom. It began within small groups of specialists and quickly spread to ever larger circles, including managers, academics, politicians, even some workers, and then to the general public. The occasional newspaper article or learned monograph grew to include hundreds, and perhaps thousands of books, lectures, seminars and pop television shows. The movement first swept the West, supposedly unreceptive to any but its own views, before conquering Asia which also decided to look East. Now, you can hardly escape it.

Fascination with Japanese-style management (*nihonteki keiei*) is quite different from most management fads which have had a tendency to flare up suddenly and are then quickly forgotten. This intense interest has been around for quite some time, certainly since the 1950s, and it should be with us for many more years, surely well into the 21st century. Moreover, as noted, it has attracted the attention of a much wider audience. That Japanese management is not just a simple formula or list of infallible principles is also to the good. The more people study Japanese management, the more they find of use. Thus, the focus has broadened to comprise ever more facets, from QC to *kanban* and from *zen* to *kaizen*.

Just as significant, the movement has become increasingly serious rather than increasingly frivolous. Initially, much of the interest in Japanese management was mere curiosity. Look how the Japanese do things! Isn't it intriguing (if not quaint)? But this inquisitiveness was soon replaced by concern and anxiety as Japanese companies won out in sector after sector and the Japanese economy became the most powerful in the world. Now the desire is emulation. What can we learn from the Japanese? What can they teach us so that we may manage our personnel better and make our companies more competitive?

It is for these very reasons that the movement is widespread, that it is gaining in depth, that it influences more people, and that one must be more cautious than before about how it is propagated and what it pretends to be. New intellectual movements always elevate false prophets as well as profiteers, those who gain from spreading what may be little more than illusions and myths. In fact, some may engage in a little myth making on the side.

One grave cause for concern is that so much of what one reads or hears about Japanese management—outside of Japan—is positive. There is a general consensus on the excellence of one practice or another or the system as a whole. Prominent foreign *gurus*, from Deming and Drucker to Ouchi and Pascale have sought to inculcate respect for the Japanese way of doing certain things. Few schools of business are without their in-house "experts" who tutor students on all sorts of Japanese wizardry. The treatment is equally favorable in most popular magazines and even made it big on television. "If Japan can, why can't we?," became the refrain.

There were admittedly some quibblers, myself included, but the majority of the supposed "experts" were solidly in the Japanese camp.[1] They felt that its system was admirable and eminently worthy of emulation. Not only was the overall tone positive in their writings, but there also were amazingly few references to any accompanying defects or drawbacks to the various management techniques. Rare were any mentions of setbacks for major Japanese companies. Indeed, most of the case studies just reinforced the idea that the Japanese are bound to succeed.

To make Japanese management look even better, many of the authors and speakers adopted a very different approach to Western management. It was regularly run down and decried. Its flaws and failings were broadly demonstrated. The setbacks were dramatized. Examples of failures were used to "prove" how poorly Western companies performed, especially when facing Japanese competitors.

The result was a bizarre contest between an idealized and expurgated Japanese system and a debased and unflattering caricature of the Western system. The Japanese treasured the individual worker and sought his participation; Western managers treated workers like objects and just gave orders. Japan offered job security and even lifetime employment; in the West, companies engaged in hire and fire. Japanese workers donned neat uniforms and engaged in quality control; Americans wore greasy jeans and left Coke bottles in auto frames. William Ouchi went so far as to claim that "the American model is the opposite of the Japanese model in every important respect," and then proceeded to clarify that this was not in America's favor.[2]

Of course, we all know the debasement of Western management styles is an exaggeration. Many American and European companies have as much concern for their workers as any in Japan, sometimes more. Western companies also show an interest in quality. And, according to statistics, job security is often as high in the West as in Japan. Oddly enough, it was not a foreigner but a Japanese, Kazuo Koike, who sought to demystify the notion that Japan was systematically different from the rest of the world.[3]

The daily workings of the Japanese system are less well-known. First of all, in actuality, many books on the subject merely portray a collection of myths bearing little relation to reality. The Japanese system as it actually exists is nowhere near the paragon of perfection as claimed. While there is certainly room for admiration and emulation, when reduced to its true dimensions, the Japanese method of management has its problems as well. Most certainly, there is also considerably more room for criticism.

It is hard to grasp just how the "Japanapologists" managed to pull off this hoax. Nearly everyone knows that there is no perfect, or even model, management system in the world. They must all have weaknesses and defects. Every human endeavor does. Thus, this glorification of Japan should have caused more people to wonder whether the "hype" was not greatly overdone.

For anyone familiar with the Japanese attitude toward Japanese management, the success of this myth making is even stranger. For, in Japan, where people have a first-hand acquaintance with the system, there is plenty of criticism. In fact, there is an almost unending round of censure of one sort or another from one quarter or another. There, Western "experts" would be scorned if it were not assumed that they simply did not know what they were talking about. As it happens, most Western books on Japanese management elicit more laughter than applause.

For instance, characteristics highly praised in the West have been much criticized by ordinary Japanese employees. The career escalator, lifetime employment, and QC are not without their Japanese detractors. Even managers, who benefit most from the system, do not like all aspects and certainly feel that some are under such strain that they must be revamped or scrapped. As for top executives, though they may laud Japanese practices to foreign visitors, they belong to various committees and think tanks that seek far-reaching reforms of the system.

Japanese literature itself is full of negative references and criticisms[4]—not only in academic works on the subject, few of which go to the lengths of adulation of foreign books, but also in more popular media. The daily press is full of investigations and exposés which show that the system is lacking or creates unwanted problems. It also regularly reproduces letters to editors from irate employees. This dissatisfaction is expressed in formal surveys undertaken by the government, private companies, specialized institutes, and the media. But it comes out most clearly in the gripes and complaints of workers and managers alike when they go out drinking after work.

It would seem that the only ones enamored of the Japanese management system are foreigners—not Japanese. And, of all the foreigners, those who seem to know the least about the realities of the system are those who write or lecture most extensively on the subject and are supposed to be "experts."

Why is this so? It would seem that foreign experts have dreadfully little hands-on familiarity with Japan. Most have never lived there. They have never run a company there. They have never even worked for a company there.[5] Usually, they have merely made one or more quick trips and derive most of their learning from what they read   by other equally uninformed foreign observers.

The case of other "experts" who live, work, and even run companies in Japan is still more puzzling. Some are business consultants who have constant daily contact with managers and workers while others are academics who teach business courses attended by Japanese students. They cannot possibly be unaware of the problems and crises that arise. In fact, they are paid to figure out what is wrong. And, if they read the daily papers, they must know that plenty is wrong.

Yet, many foreign "experts" only want to show what is good about the system. Perhaps they do this to protect their reputation as experts; to have more people read their books or attend their lectures; to earn more money in seminars or consulting practices; or even to be subsidized by Japanese bodies that liberally spread money among those who promote a positive image of the country. It is easier to become famous and rich by spreading the gospel of Japanese management. Critics, like myself, attract much less attention and fewer fees. This is particularly true of academics and consultants who base their career on the ability to sell one technique or another that supposedly guarantees commercial success to those who apply it. In other cases, reputations have been built on ideas that show the Japanese have grown strong by adopting a technique initially offered at home. While shunned in the U.S., for instance, it was supposedly taken up with alacrity by the Japanese.

One interesting case is Ouchi's Theory Z. The Japanese must have been amazed to learn that, although they had never heard of it before, they had been practicing it all along since "other facets of lifetime employment—such as trust, loyalty to a firm, and commitment to a job over most of one's productive years—are the foundation of Theory Z."[6] Deming's claim of contributing to Japan's success is much more credible, as long as you assume that what they practice is really what he preached. He was also more genuine in his affection for his favorite pupil Japan than the others, many of whom would peddle Martian business practices if that would do the trick. Thus, Deming warned the Japanese:

> It is important that Japanese management remain strong, not weakened and diluted by adoption of some of the practices that are largely responsible for the decline of Western industry. It is possible for a strong body to become infected, to become weak. Japanese management has responsibilities to continue to be strong and not to pick up infections from Western management.[7]

Many explanations of the tidal wave of foreign mythmaking would be endorsed by Japanese critics of the system. They do not much like foreign experts or think highly of their expertise. One of Japan's leading industrial sociologists, who basically approves of the system, poses yet another intriguing theory. He feels that foreigners praise the system to make the Japanese overlook the defects and thus fail to reform it. This would make our management experts even more devious in spreading the foreign myth of Japanese management. According to Kunio Odaka:

> Over the last twenty years, the myth has escalated and proliferated to create a dangerous situation, especially in Japan. Originally couched in a foreign language, deviating from the reality of Japanese management in several particulars, and tending to praise the good side and ignore the bad, the myth is today finding eager converts among Japanese who use it to justify exaggerated displays of national pride. The situation tends to hide the true nature of Japanese management and to interfere with efforts to correct its by-now conspicuous defects.[8]

Balancing the Good and the Bad

If such mythification is dangerous for the Japanese, it is at least equally perilous for the rest of us, especially those who unsuspectingly believe it.

For purely intellectual reasons, it is essential to be aware of the bad and good sides of anything if one is to understand how it operates, what it achieves, what its impact is. Knowing only the positive aspects of Japanese management, while ignoring the negative ones, would leave an observer with a very faulty and inaccurate view of the system. It would be even more difficult, then, to understand why so many Japanese are dissatisfied with it.

It would be even more dangerous to see only half of the picture if one actually has to live with the system. Numerous foreigners either want to enter or have already joined Japanese companies because they believe the system is so congenial. They hope to benefit from its many advantages. And, they intend to make the system work for them. Imagine their surprise when they find some of the advantages lacking, or at least grossly overestimated, while drawbacks proliferate. This surprise quickly turns into frustration and anger.

Better knowledge of the system, its opportunities and drawbacks, is even more important for businessmen who want to incorporate some of Japan's supposedly superior techniques at home. They pick techniques on the basis of reports about their virtues. They would naturally be disturbed to find that there are also vices to those techniques or that the system as a whole is flawed. Better they should know just what to expect so that they do not pick the wrong aspects or expect to accomplish more than is possible.

Those who have to compete against the Japanese are in a particularly critical situation and under greater pressure. They have to contend with extremely capable players, among the toughest they have ever faced, so they must know just what makes them tick. They have to know the strengths, to watch out for them and avoid damage. They have to know the weaknesses as well, so that they can fight back with a greater chance of winning. Above all, they should not be overawed by an unjustified reputation for all-around excellence when that is not the case. There are chinks in the armor, and they must be found.

Still, while this book will stress the weaknesses and failings of Japanese management, it is by no means an attempt to belittle or run down the Japanese. The next chapter will deal with some of the strengths and yet others will be mentioned further on. The Japanese are, indeed, daunting rivals and overlooking their strengths would be as foolhardy as neglecting their weaknesses. A detailed discussion of the strengths of the Japanese system is not presented here as existing literature is replete with such material.

To tell the other side of the story, this book must first disaggregate. The Japanese "system" consists of many different methods and techniques, some of which succeed marvelously while others fail miserably. By separating, rather than mixing, it becomes much easier to spotlight the strengths and weaknesses.

One discrete area, which is dealt with in the next chapter, involves the "hard," more mechanical aspects of factory management. These are things done by technicians in order to boost the productivity of the physical plant. They include such things as plant layout, determination of scale, acquisition of machinery and equipment, automation and robotization, inventory control and delivery of parts. This has, on the whole, been a successful sphere of operation and its significance has actually been under-estimated by most.

Far more attention is focused on the "soft" aspects of management—managing people rather than things, sometimes which occurs in the factory. Among the more useful techniques employed by the Japanese are quality control, suggestion boxes, worker participation in productivity enhancement and, theoretically at least, management. On the whole, this is quite successful even if it does occasionally place an undue burden on the workers.

Nothing, however, has received greater acclaim than the "soft" management at higher levels for white-collar employees in the company's offices and administration—those known as the *sararimen* or "salarymen." Among the techniques used are *ringisho* and bottom-up decision-making, meetings and *nemawashi*, job rotation, teamwork, the career escalator for promotions and lifetime employment. Oddly enough, this is where praise for the system is most overblown and, in truth, the worst failings are to be found.

Finally, there is the question of business strategy as defined by top executives. This consists of plans for expansion, diversification, product development, and so on. It also involves, incidentally but very significantly, the quest for market share as opposed to profits.

Once we separate out the various aspects of Japanese management, their methods work will become more evident than when everything was mixed together in a meaningless hodgepodge.

First and foremost, we must avoid the tendency to assume that all aspects of Japanese-style management apply everywhere. For example, quality control is largely restricted to ordinary workers in the factories and it is much less practiced by office workers or top executives. Bottom-up decision-making, *ringisho*, and the like are basically circumscribed to the offices or white-collar workers. They barely exist among blue-collar workers who tend to follow orders. Both categories engage in job rotation, but factory workers merely move from one production job to the next as required while the salarymen progress from one type of job to another as part of a career path.

Secondly, as has already been suggested, the Japanese have been more successful in some spheres than others. They accomplish the most with things, not people, and their layout, automation, etc. are second to none. They also do fairly well with people at lower levels, namely with blue-collar workers in factories who, since they are further down, could readily be dictated to more than consulted. They have fared less well in handling white-collar employees, namely those slated to rise in the hierarchy and who have to be consulted. Japanese management has a miserable record with women at every level.

What is yet more interesting is that even where the Japanese perform reasonably well, there have been defects and imperfections. Thus, while quality control works out nicely for blue-collar staff, it creates some frustration if overdone. Even for a relatively straightforward matter like just-in-time delivery, there are unexpected complications and costs. When it comes to the urge for market share, where the Japanese score highly, it is important to remember that the constant striving for increased market share is often done at the expense of profits.

It is also necessary to look at different economic sectors separately. Some management techniques are applied selectively. In fact, while most are used in manufacturing and some soft ones in advanced services, there is little to be seen of the marvels of Japanese management in more backward services, distribution, agriculture, and even parts of manufacturing.

Thus, it is valuable to examine each aspect individually, to seek the good and the bad, to determine which facets are positive and which negative. Once this is done, the Japanese record not only becomes less admirable, it is very spotty. Even amidst the good there are definite flaws and it is not safe to assume that any one technique or practice is successful no matter what the rest of the system may be.

The Management Myth

Views on just what Japanese management consists of, and what its most significant features are, vary from one observer to the next. Like the three blind men, the experts face the elephant from different places and do not always touch the same part. Still, there is a certain consensus on the core—what the Japanese have come to call the "three sacred treasures"—lifetime employment, seniority wages and promotion, and enterprise unionism. Sometimes a fourth is added—company welfare benefits. James Abegglen, one of the pioneers of the movement, neatly explains:

> ... the truly distinctive features of Japanese management methods compared to management methods in other countries are largely in the area of personnel relations—in the recruiting, compensating, and organization of personnel, and in their own organization into labor unions. This includes the often cited features of career employment, seniority-based pay and promotion, and the enterprise union. Most of the other special features of Japanese management—such as the absence of mergers or acquisitions, the emphasis on internal training, and the tendency for the employee to identify with the company as a whole rather than with his or her skill category—stem from these basic special features.[9]

These three features form the basic pillars for the assorted practices and techniques that are widely admired. Because workers are recruited for a "lifetime," they can be trained at company expense. Because they depend on the company, and it on them, there is no need for aggressive labor unions to defend their rights. Because they actively compete with other companies, it is in the workers' own interest to improve quality, raise productivity and even, on occasion, to accept smaller wage increments. Indeed, the more enthusiastic supporters paint a picture in which hardly anything can disturb relations between labor and management and harmony and loyalty seem perfectly natural. This notion was expressed by Gene Gregory, a professor of Japanese management, among many others:

> Workers and managers alike identify themselves with the goals of the enterprise, and their most important identification is, reciprocally, the name of the company for which they work. They belong to the enterprise in the same sense they belong to a family and, as in the family, a living reciprocity of obligations and rewards binds them to the enterprise in common destiny. As they are strongly identified with it as well as by the goals of enterprise, members are moved all the more strongly to try to improve it.[10]

This idyllic version of Japanese management is unfortunately subject to question from several directions. Here, only the principal themes will be discussed. More detailed examinations of Japanese management will be undertaken in other sections.

The first question, of course, is whether Japanese management really practices what its proponants claim. Are employees really recruited for a "lifetime" stint? Is promotion and remuneration really based on years of service? Do workers feel that their identity is so closely linked to that of the company that they happily make any necessary sacrifices? Do they actually like the system? Do they have any objections to the system?

Over the years, lifetime employment has become a firm anchor in many foreigners' vision of Japanese management. In Japan, however, it has been disputed ever since it was proposed by Dr. Abegglen as the "critical difference" in *The Japanese Factory.*[11] Witness the unemployment rate among many older Japanese people and it becomes evident that they were not hired for life. Other aspects are also challenged as incorrect or greatly exaggerated by Japanese specialists, and not only those on the left.[12] A closer look at the practical realities should be enough to turn the balance against the notion that Japanese management behaves in practice as it is supposed to in theory.

The next question is whether or not the various Japanese management practices are "Japanese." That is, whether the behavior is inherently Japanese and largely alien to others or simply Japanese variations on common cultural themes. Those who laud Japanese management, especially from the cultural angle, claim that there is something special about Japanese society and people which leads them to behave in ways that are remarkably different from foreigners. While this view is quite pleasing to those Japanese who enjoy being seen as "unique," some similarities can be found abroad. Certain foreign companies also keep employees for a very long time, base wages and promotion to a certain degree on seniority, and encourage greater identity between labor and management. Other techniques, some of them originally borrowed from the West, are relatively neutral, such as quality control, industrial engineering, in-house training, etc.

But even the "three treasures" may not be that specific to Japan if one ignores other aspects, such as the role of skill formation. Then, according to Kazuo Koike, professor of economics at the Kyoto Institute of Economic Research:

> . . . reality is distorted and we have the illusions of "permanent employment," "seniority wages" and "enterprise-based labor unions." The consequent belief that these conditions are totally dissimilar to labor management practices in the West is enshrined in the culturalist thesis. This thesis in effect suggests that the Japanese mentality—and thereby its culture—is unique. The purpose of this book is, in short, to present sustainable arguments against the culturalist thesis.[13]

This is done with abundant statistics and case studies from Europe and the United States.[14] Admittedly, the American system is often quite different from the Japanese and one can readily imagine why American academics must see the Japanese system as rather "special." But European companies are often closer to the middle, so that the American system can be regarded as no less extreme than the Japanese. To which it might be added that emerging Asian companies are also in between, a mixture of the "modern" Western and more "traditional" Japanese approaches, although what appears as "Japanese" frequently derives from their own culture.

By the way, this supposedly "traditional" Japanese system, which allegedly has its roots in ancient Japanese habits and customs, is actually quite modern. It did not exist in Meiji days, it did not exist in prewar days, it was only created after the war under the unusual circumstances of those years. This is widely known by the Japanese who readily demonstrate that in earlier times there was enormous job mobility, workers showed hardly any loyalty, once they had acquired new skills they moved on to new employers who would reward them better. Trade unions were often quite aggressive, strikes were violent, and absenteeism was rife.[15] Harmony was the exception and, at most, a goal mouthed by company managers who were frustrated by the action of their employees.[16]

Nonetheless, because the country was so poor and devastated after the war, and urgently had to restore the economy, there was more need for cooperation and compromise. Workers wanted job security or they would starve. Employers wanted a steady labor force first to improve quality and then, as the period of rapid growth began, to bring on the workers who would be needed for expansion. The economic boom permitted employers to hire unskilled recruits and train them for jobs which might be required in the future. And they would hardly think of firing anyone when ever more workers were sought. With production increasing, exports expanding, and income rising, it was easier to provide both management and labor with what they wanted.

These conditions were very propitious for "lifetime" employment and other Japanese practices. Indeed, there would have been a similar effect wherever such conditions prevailed. But now, with slower growth, the situation has changed and the system is being put under much greater strains than ever. That it worked in the 1960s was not terribly surprising. Whether it will still work in the 1990s remains to be seen.

Moreover, it should never be forgotten that the supposedly "typical" Japanese system, the one regularly presented abroad as the true essence of Japanese management, actually only applies to part of the economy. It is most prevalent in big companies, especially in manufacturing and some advanced services. It is basically lacking in smaller companies, in particular among lesser suppliers, subcontractors, and establishments in distribution and more backward services. Thus, the "typical" system only prevails in a few percent of the companies with perhaps a third of all workers and, even there, it does not include everybody.[17]

One may well ask what the management of these smaller companies is like? Actually, it is probably closer to the ill-reputed Western system than the highly touted Japanese style. Little can be seen of the "sacred treasures." There is less lifetime employment than hire and fire as necessary. Promotion depends more on the whims of company owners and managers. There are very few unions of any sort. Welfare frills are sorely lacking. In addition, workers put in longer hours, under more painful conditions, for lower wages.[18] But this is not entirely the fault of the smaller companies. They do not have much choice since they are often used as buffers by larger ones.

The "typical" system is therefore more "atypical" than its admirers would normally concede, although every Japanese knows this for a fact. "The myth would have us believe that these Japanese management practices are widespread at all Japanese firms regardless of size," complains Odaka.[19] Still, the myth persists as the large, dynamic Japanese companies most foreigners deal with do apply the system. And even the smaller or more backward companies at least aspire to implement the "three treasures." ■

Notes

1. Among the few truly critical works were S. Prakash Sethi, Nobuaki Namiki, and Carl L. Swanson, *The False Promise of the Japanese Miracle*, and Jon Woronoff, *Japan's Wasted Workers*, first edition. Among the more fervent admirers were William Ouchi, *Theory Z*, Richard Tanner Pascale, and Anthony G. Athos, *The Art of Japanese Management*, and Ezra F. Vogel, *Japan as Number One*.

2. Ouchi, op. cit., p. 58.

3. See Kazuko Koike, *Understanding Industrial Relations in Modern Japan*.

4. Some of the Japanese writers will be referred to in later sections. Most comprehensive and lucid is Kunio Odaka's *Japanese Management: A Forward-Looking Analysis*. Distinctly less constructive are numerous "Marxist" commentators, including Shigeyoshi Tokunaga, "A Marxist Interpretation of Japanese Industrial Relations," in Taishiro Shirai ed., *Contemporary Industrial Relations in Japan*, pp. 313-330.

5. This applies most strongly to the authors of books on management. Those dealing with industrial relations usually at least engaged in field work. Most interesting are books by authors who worked in Japanese companies, like Robert E. Cole, *Japanese Blue Collar*, Rodney Clark, *The Japanese Company*, Satoshi Kamata, *Japan In The Passing Lane*, Dorinne

Kondo, *Crafting Selves,* and Thomas P. Rohlen, *For Harmony and Strength.*

6. Ouchi, op. cit., p. 25.

7. Mary Walton, *The Deming Management Method,* p. 248.

8. Odaka, op. cit., p. i-ii.

9. James C. Abegglen, *The Strategy of Japanese Business,* p. 80.

10. Gene Gregory, "The Logic of Japanese Enterprise," in Japan Productivity Center, *Strategies for Productivity,* p. 117.

11. Abegglen, *The Japanese Factory,* p. 130.

12. Odaka, op. cit., Mikio Sumiya, *The Japanese Industrial Relations Reconsidered,* and others.

13. Koike, op. cit., p. 1.

14. For further details, see Koike, op. cit.

15. See Sumiya, op. cit.

16. See W. Dean Kinzley, *Industrial Harmony in Modern Japan, The Invention of a Tradition.*

17. See Jon Woronoff, *Japan: The (Coming) Economic Crisis.*

18. On smaller companies and the lot of non-regular workers, see Norma J. Chalmers, *Industrial Relations in Japan, The Peripheral Workforce,* Kondo, op. cit., and Michael J. Smitka, *Competitive Ties, Subcontracting in the Japanese Automotive Industry.*

19. Odaka, op. cit., p. 7.

2

Onward ... If Not Always Upward

Getting Your Bearings

■ As stated, the purpose of this book is not to belittle or denigrate Japanese-style management. It has many fine features that are worthy of praise and which will be lauded here. In fact, this chapter is devoted specifically to a number of the more successful aspects of the Japanese management system. Some of them relate to the management of people, specifically, blue-collar workers and those in Japan's better factories. Other aspects worthy of praise are the "harder," more mechanical management techniques, involved in the creation of those factories. Also, top management's primary task which, in Japan, is not enhancing profitability but expanding production and boosting market share will also be examined.

The bigger picture, on the whole, is equally positive. Productivity has risen more rapidly and effectively, and also over an amazingly long time, by using some of the techniques which will be examined here. Japan, or at least the manufacturing sector, provides an exceptional example of how productivity can be given the highest priority in a society which realizes that it is crucial to economic development in general. This economic development, by the way, is also examplary. Japan has repeatedly outperformed older, better-endowed countries and still keeps advancing.

This said, it must be conceded that many of the greater achievements lie in the past, back in the 1950s and 1960s and not the 1980s. It is rather unlikely that the 1990s will witness a new burst of speed although, even while maturing, the economy should hold up fairly well and productivity continue to grow. Japan will also build new factories, create new products, develop brilliant new technologies, and continue to astonish us all. Still, it would be foolish to forget that the truly exceptional period was some decades ago.

The idea of growing and then slowing is easy enough to grasp. Everybody matures and slows down. But there is another concept which is even more important in judging Japan's achievements. It is much subtler but its impact is even greater. The problem is that it can work both ways, for good and bad. For some of Japan's finer features, those which are eminently praiseworthy under ordinary circumstances, become much less so when the Japanese exaggerate. This has to be mentioned because the Japanese frequently do exaggerate. They will find a promising management technique, product, or sector and push it for all it is worth, only to discover that beyond a certain point there are not only diminishing but negative returns.

This can best be illustrated by referring to another aspect that is receiving increasing attention, namely *gambare*. It is both a technique for managing people and for heightening the intensity of other techniques. And it pervades the business community. *Gambare* means to persevere or endure. In colloquial translation, it might be conveyed as "hang in there" or "never say die." So it is not inscrutable to foreigners. But it has much deeper roots in Japan, being much favored by the ancient *samurai* warriors and still inculcated today. According to Benjamin Duke, in describing the Japanese school system, "*gambare*: persevere, endure, don't give up! is integral to being Japanese."[1]

Gambare is not just an ancient cultural trait, it was picked up and used by companies. Factory walls are covered with banners that tout assorted *gambare* slogans, after a pep talk the manager will say "*gambare*" to his underlings, and in one Mazda plant fathers were urged to work hard and diligently by their children's drawings on the theme of *gambare*.[2] On the face of it, *gambare* is a very useful trait and one that can certainly invigorate a company. It can unite workers and make them strive for common goals. In practice, it has allowed Honda to expand, Sony to lead technologically, and Japan to beat the West in many ways.

But one cannot stop there. Like so many other Japanese techniques, cultural characteristics, and supposed virtues, *gambare* has a flip side. The urge to persevere, to endure, to accomplish a goal come what may becomes emotional and, when it does, it displaces more rational thoughts as to what the cost is, what the odds are, what the real chances of winning may be. That is already a strike against it.

If, as sometimes happens, the costs are not only high but continue mounting, it may be wisest not to persevere. If the odds against winning are steep enough, maybe one should not endure but rather withdraw from the fray. If there is really no chance of succeeding, it is doubtlessly best to pull back and cut costs. But *gambare* makes the Japanese push too hard and too far. When they finally realize that it was a mistake, they are then blocked from admitting it by another cultural tick, that old acquaintance "saving face."

Thus, in practice, Japanese companies have frequently expanded production too much, gotten into sectors for which they were not really equipped, opened more subsidiaries than they could efficiently run, and taken on opponents they could not beat. Within their own companies, as will soon become apparent, they have turned wonderful techniques and methods into sources of frustration and tools of oppression. Seen in this light, it is much harder to speak unreservedly of "success."

Factories Foremost

Where the Japanese have shown uncommon ability and ingenuity is in operating factories. This applies both to "hard" aspects, like plant design, selection of machinery, economies of scale, and "soft" ones, namely how factory workers are managed. This success has attracted the attention of many foreign academics, managers, workers, and even the general public. It has been written about extensively and much of what is said is valid and worthy of praise—up to a point.[3]

First, the hard aspects. When the Japanese build a plant, more often than elsewhere it is a completely new plant, or greenfield facility. This was quite normal just after the war, since existing factories had been demolished or were hopelessly obsolete. But it has continued since. Even when existing facilities could be revamped, the tendency is greater to start from scratch.

In so doing, there is usually a strong emphasis on scale. The plant should be sufficiently large to produce in vast quantities and thereby lower unit costs. Sometimes the decision on size is rational, i.e. based on careful estimates of potential sales. Often enough, such estimates are flawed or non-existent, mainly but not only for new, untried products. To play it safe, unlike many foreign companies which would prefer being on the low side, Japanese ambitiously shoot for the high side. The *gambare* spirit takes over. Scale is increased even more if it is known that competitors are building as big or bigger plants.

Within the plants, the layout is first-rate. Every machine is in the right place to facilitate the flow and make it easier for workers to get their jobs done quickly and precisely. The industrial engineering is tip top and the time-and-motion boys get movements down to the split second. In all this, the Japanese tend to cut operations up into small enough pieces that they can be easily performed almost automatically by workers even if they occasionally put a few together again for work enlargement.

As for equipment, it is the very latest and most efficient. This machinery can often perform more functions than that found elsewhere, which makes the whole line more flexible. Automation is pushed to the hilt. And robots are used to a far greater extent than abroad.[4] Whenever a job can be automated, robotized, or computerized, it is. There are few complaints because workers are usually transferred to other jobs, other facilities, or other companies. But, even if there were complaints, that would not stop the ceaseless rationalization.

Another interesting technique involves inventory control, critical for the Japanese because land is so scarce and costly. Thus, if parts or sub-units can be delivered on short notice, they can be stored less and save on inventory. Even better, if they are delivered to the assembly line as they are needed or "just-in-time," inventory costs can be slashed drastically. This *kanban* system obviously requires close cooperation with the suppliers who produce the parts.

There is no question that the *kanban* system has saved the assemblers lots of money. It also allowed them to keep closer watch over what the suppliers are doing. But it is absurd to praise Toyota, which invented the technique, or other major assemblers, for any success.[5] Most of the burden was borne by the suppliers who had to produce what was wanted when it was wanted and get it to the assembly line on time. They were stuck with arranging and rearranging their production schedule and seeing to it that trucks were ready to transport it when needed. Failure to do so inconvenienced the assembler. For the supplier, the fate was considerably worse, an end to contracts and perhaps even bankruptcy.[6]

Certainly, the Japanese have done an exceptional job on all this. They deserve whatever praise they get. Anyone who has visited Japanese factories and compared them to counterparts abroad realizes that the Japanese ones are vastly more productive. But it would be mistaken to assume that there are no drawbacks. All of this is costly, extremely costly. And any money that went into plant and equipment naturally had to be withheld from other uses such as more advertising, R&D, wages, etc.

This would not matter so much if the original choices were sober and purposeful. Then the company could compete better and earn more money. Alas, with alarming frequency, the Japanese put up factories that used too much sophisticated paraphernalia while scrapping still quite useable older facilities. That was just wasteful. Worse was the tendency toward excessive scale. If scale is too big, and goods cannot be sold, then production runs must be cut back and this again implies waste. Indeed, handling small runs in a big plant can be more expensive than handling larger runs in a plant somewhat too small. Worse, if rather than cut back output, the company decides to produce to the larger scale and then tries to sell the excess production, prices will have to be lowered and profits will come down or turn into losses.

Still, what with one thing and another, there is no doubt that these achievements contributed mightily to the rise of Japanese industry. They also made a major contribution to productivity. Indeed, the hard aspects clearly added more to productivity than the softer, people-management aspects which got the most praise. This was generally agreed by Japanese productivity specialists, including Hajime Ohta, who noted that "the large increase in labor productivity improvement in the 1960s and early 1970s is largely attributable to the increase in capital investment that resulted in more equipment per worker."[7]

The story on quality control has been recited much too often to bother repeating it here. The method was developed by William Edwards Deming and others in the U.S. but was neglected.[8] The Japanese latched on to it as a way of reviving the war-torn economy. Not only did they stress quality to overcome very evident failings at the time, they brought the workers into the process. Quality was too important to be left only to inspectors and supervisors. Each worker had to do his utmost to ensure his own quality and, more important, contribute to improving quality overall.

Where the Japanese innovated most was by increasing worker participation. This was done through Quality Control Circles which proliferated rapidly.[9] They were small groups of colleagues, accustomed to working together, who would pick their own leader and examine their own activities to see what improvements could be made. These groups were not expected to chitchat idly or even brainstorm but to adopt a scientific approach to improve quality. Much was made of production statistics and graphs with an aim both to reducing defects and limiting the variations of any that remained.

Meanwhile, workers were encouraged to make suggestions. Nobody knew the job better than they and they were expected to suggest how they might accomplish yet more. These suggestions would be placed in a handy box, then examined by qualified specialists and, if truly useful, put into practice not only for that worker but wherever it applied. The worker would usually be rewarded modestly, with much honor, little money.

This was gradually absorbed into broader productivity campaigns with QC Circles working on suitable themes and individuals making appropriate suggestions.[10] They could take on a festive and competitive tone with QC Circles within a given factory, or among the company's various factories, or even nation-wide, competing for the best projects. The winners received, you guessed it, a Deming Prize. Those who made more suggestions, or smarter suggestions, or saved the company the most money, would also win prizes. Meanwhile, the workplace would be draped with banners urging everybody on to increase productivity. *Gambare!*

This being the Japanese, there was no end to it. One QC project ran into another, suggestions were expected continually, and everybody strained to raise quality and productivity a notch. The endless effort to improve and perfect was summed up as *kaizen* (continuous improvement), another Japanese practice that has become fashionable of late.[11] Thus, for example, the demand for fewer defects would be tightened to a demand for zero defects (even though everybody knew that was impossible) or more practically the target would be lowered from, say, five defects per thousand to two, and then one, and from so many defects per thousand to so many per million.

What is intriguing is that the Japanese managed to obtain considerable involvement from the workers.[12] Indeed, they even appeared to achieve some degree of acceptance of the idea that everybody was in the same boat and had to help the company. In return, supervisors became somewhat less remote and haughty than before and tended to wear the same uniform as ordinary staff. The top brass also ate in the same canteen and used the same parking lot. All workers would meet early in the morning for calisthenics, sing the company song, and have a drink together in the evening or attend the company picnic with the whole family.

This really went over big with foreign admirers. It apparently showed greater concern for the human being, the whole person, who was treated more as an equal unlike in the West where workers were just treated as objects. This "consensual, participative" bent is what made Japanese companies honorary Type Z organizations. Here Bill Ouchi elaborates on what is involved:

> Type Z companies generally show broad concern for the welfare of subordinates and co-workers as a natural part of a working relationship. Relationships between people tend to be informal and to emphasize that whole people deal with one another at work, rather than just managers with workers and clerks with machinists. This wholistic orientation, a central feature of the organization, inevitably maintains a strong egalitarian atmosphere that is a feature of all Type Z organizations.[13]

Admittedly, as I readily concede, in these areas the Japanese have achievements they can be proud of and which certainly set them above most foreign competitors. But that is no excuse for ignoring unpleasant realities or overlooking drawbacks, as so often happens. Many of these drawbacks, by the way, can be traced directly to the supposed virtue of constantly pushing further, seeking greater perfection, as in *kaizen*. This is only worse when compounded with the *gambare* spirit, in which normal limitations are ignored or flaunted.

Thus, for example, quality control and productivity drives steadily intensified. There were ever more projects, they became increasingly more difficult and circle members were under heightened pressure to succeed. Those who did not participate actively enough were subject to severe criticism. For suggestions, the situation became almost absurd, with companies competing to see which could generate the most. Some claimed to get a thousand per employee each year and to implement most of them.[14] It is hard to believe that so many improvements could be made and, if they were, the shop floor must have been in constant turmoil.

This same tendency to exaggerate reduced the *kanban* system to a caricature. At first, orders were placed a month in advance, leaving suppliers plenty of time to comply. Then the lead was decreased to two weeks, then a week, then sometimes a few days. Meanwhile, deliveries, which had been once a month or once a week were tightened to once every few days or to every single day. Trucks which used to carry full loads were soon carrying partial loads or traveling nearly empty just to deliver in time. Whatever the savings on inventory, there were now additional and mounting costs for transport and, just as bad, busier traffic on the roads, lack of parking space, and more pollution.

Equality and harmony came under even greater pressure. The first QC Circles probably were spontaneous and, even if not, workers were happy to get together after hours and to be consulted by management. But there was soon nothing voluntary about them. Everybody had to join the QC Circle and no excuse was acceptable for absences. Members had to participate actively and were rated on their participation. The team leader was increasingly not a fellow worker but a supervisor who had to report back to the official quality control hierarchy and see to it that his group did not fall behind. Making suggestions was equally compulsive. Quotas were imposed and any worker who did not make enough (good) suggestions was in trouble. So much for Deming's philosophy and principles like "eliminate slogans, exhortations and targets for the workforce."

Any equality, by the way, was always a bit fictitious. While everyone wore the same uniform and badge, certain workers wore different caps or bands so you could tell them apart. As for supervisors, everyone knew who they were just by noting that they were older (and not toiling on the assembly line). The idea that ordinary workers felt an affinity with the boss, aside from some few remaining founders, was rather far-fetched.[15] They only saw him once or twice a year for some special celebration or founder's day. Even when executives had lunch in the same canteen, parked in the same lot, or attended the same party, everybody knew that they dined in fancy restaurants (at company expense), drove bigger cars (or had chauffeur-driven ones), and retired to much more comfortable homes (often subsidized by the company).

As for bottom-up decision-making in the factory, there was not even a pretense of that for ordinary workers. That much could be gathered from their conversations and grievances. Just how little they were consulted can be sensed from the following excerpt in the diary of a Japanese investigative reporter who worked in a Toyota factory:

> Whenever we get together these days, all we talk about is the changing of the work shifts. There's a rumor that next year the present two-shift system, in which one shift immediately follows the other, will be dropped for separate day and night shifts, with some hours in between. But no official announcement has been made. The foreman himself hasn't received any information. The projected system is designed to get more overtime out of everyone, and most of us are against it, but as someone said, "If it's official management policy, then there's nothing we can do about it." The rumor is upsetting, but it's difficult to fight against a rumor. Management is following a very clever psychological strategy. Even a basic change of working conditions such as this won't be discussed in or by the labor union. In fact, nobody mentions the labor union at all. It's as if the union doesn't exist.[16]

At any rate, solidarity is hard to achieve between blue-collar workers who are usually high school graduates and white-collar workers who are mainly college graduates. Admittedly, a novice salaryman might be sent for a stint on the assembly line to see what it's like and what his company produces. But it is usually not for long. And everyone knows that he is slated to rise much faster. The existing distinction between blue-collar and white-collar workers, factory and office workers, only increases as companies maintain headquarters in Tokyo or other larger cities and locate their factories in small towns and remote prefectures. The two hardly ever mingle any more.

The only way workers could have enjoyed anything resembling equality with supervisors or executives would have been through an active role of the trade union. That could, at least, have evened out the power relationship somewhat. But it was always clear that the equality and harmony were based on concessions of the company and not rights won by the workers. Any attempt to reverse the situation, by activating the union and making more stringent demands, was bitterly fought by management.[17] To add insult to injury, workers were then accused of disturbing the "harmonious" relationship and poorly rewarding management for its show of concern. So much for equality, harmony, and wholistic relations!

From Productivity Hero to Has-Been

Another achievement for which Japan is justifiably praised is the ability to boost productivity. This was accomplished, in the factory at least, by the various techniques just mentioned. They permitted labor productivity to grow by as much as 6 percent a year on the average from 1960-1988—a very fast pace compared to other countries, including most Western ones and especially the U.S., with a growth rate of a mere 1.9 percent.[18]

Part of this can be traced to the fact that, after the war, Japan was starting from a lower base. The U.S., which had been less affected—and was already much more productive—naturally improved less rapidly. But Japan also outpaced the European countries, in a more comparable position, with some 3.5 percent for OECD-Europe. Thus, Japan was raising productivity almost twice as fast as its competitors and was a true productivity hero.

However, growth rates varied considerably from 1960-1988. During the 1960s and early 1970s, the rate was a spectacular 9.4 percent. With the oil crisis, it slumped. But the slowdown was not only due to higher oil prices. Most of the easy gains, those coming from bigger plants, using newer machinery, and more advanced technology were gone. Now it was necessary for Japan to move ahead on the basis of its own innovations. With greater automation and robotization than other OECD countries, it did manage to remain a leader with 3.2 percent average annual growth from 1973-88.

But the gap was much smaller. OECD-Europe improved productivity by about 5 percent a year from 1960-73 compared to Japan's 9.4 percent and 2.3 percent from 1973-88 compared to Japan's 3.2 percent. Meanwhile, more backward countries which began industrializing, mainly in East and Southeast Asia, were catching up. They displayed the sort of growth that Japan had not seen since the 1960s.

While this progress was impressive, it was extremely spotty. It was unusually high in manufacturing, statistics from which the Japanese and their admirers most proudly cite time and again. Yet, even there, some sectors were highly productive and others were not. Those which permitted greater scale economies, larger inputs of fresh technology, and broader use of labor-saving machinery did brilliantly. The rest were lackluster. Among the leaders were steel, shipbuilding, automotive, machinery, and electronics. The laggards included textiles, garments and footwear, furniture, paper and food processing.

Moreover, big companies were much more productive than smaller ones. For example, companies with over 1,000 employees were about three times as productive as those with less than 100.[19]

That is partly because they could afford the new plants, advanced technologies, and labor-saving machinery while smaller, weaker firms could not. But there was an additional reason, one which gave them an unfair advantage. Larger companies, especially assemblers, were able to concentrate on those tasks which could be accomplished most efficiently and required the least labor. Labor-intensive, inherently inefficient, or dirty and unpleasant work was dumped on suppliers and subcontractors.[20]

In addition, even while boosting productivity on the shop floor, manufacturers did less well with other kinds of tasks. They found it harder to rationalize or modernize work in the administration, marketing, and transport of the very same products. Thus, while the number of blue-collar workers shrank and contributed to productivity, the number of associated workers such as white-collar (clerical and administrative), grey-collar (transport), and pink-collar (females doing assorted jobs) rose.

Thus, all too often, gains on the shop floor were lost elsewhere. For example, production workers were shifted to marketing, which was highly labor-intensive. Or more truck drivers were needed for just-in-time delivery, which reduced productivity. Or work was created to occupy putative managers who were not really needed but could not just be discarded. Productivity for many women, particularly those who were unnecessary or frivolous, hardly rose at all. Thus, productivity in manufacturing, which was rather exceptional, was not as good as it looked.

In other sectors, the situation was much worse. These sectors, which will be discussed in greater detail later, were numerous. In agriculture, due to limited land, even intensive farming was relatively inefficient and unproductive in economic terms. Distribution, with many layers of wholesalers and retailers, and terribly small outlets, was almost as bad. Construction, which only modernized grudgingly and remained amazingly labor-intensive, was not much better. In the services there were some fairly efficient branches, especially in the financial area. But the bulk were still backward and made exceedingly poor use of people.

So, when you consider the overall level of productivity of the whole economy and not just manufacturing, the result is nothing to brag about. This is particularly true because, no matter how outsiders may imagine Japan, manufacturing is not their largest sector. Other sectors cumulatively account for a much larger share of the labor force, some two-thirds by the 1990s. What is more disturbing is that manufacturing's share keeps declining while the service sector share rises. The low-to-modest productivity sectors predominate more and more over the one high-productivity sector.

Considered in this light, Japan's comparative position is not as good as it initially appeared. True, it has raised manufacturing productivity more rapidly, but there are many areas where it has not caught up and is still less productive than other OECD members. Even for manufacturing, it trails the U.S. by a small margin. When other sectors are included, Japan cuts a very poor figure, indeed. According to the authoritative Japan Productivity Center, in 1987 Japan was actually next-to-last in the overall labor productivity listing. While it had an index of 100, the U.S. and Canada boasted 134, France and Italy stood at 131, West Germany showed 124, and Spain 112, and even Great Britain was marginally ahead with 101.[21] See Table 2.1.

The Economy Slows Down

While many admire Japanese management for its intrinsic value, many more endorse it because it has contributed to Japan's overall economic success. In order to revive their own sluggish economies or raise growth rates yet higher, it is suggested that Japanese methods might be appropriate. After all, they contributed to one of the world's greatest economic miracles.

Table 2.1

Comparative Productivity 1987

	Japan	U.S.	Germany	France
Manufacturing	100	112	84	87
Agriculture, forestry, fishery	100	337	135	226
Construction	100	118	135	142
Wholesale and retail	100	167	137	171
Transportation and Communication	100	155	128	131
Finance, insurance, real estate	100	119	98	127
Overall	100	134	124	131

Source: Japan Productivity Center, *International Comparison of Productivity Level and Trends of 11 OECD Countries*, 1989.

There is no doubt that, once it started rebuilding the economy, Japan made exceptional progress and achieved growth rates that no other country could match. Well after it began slowing down, Japan appeared to get through various recessions and the oil crises better than most. Even today, it keeps chugging along at an enviable rate. Meanwhile, the average income has risen steadily so that by now Japanese earn more than Americans and most Europeans.

Still, to understand the situation, it is necessary to take a closer look at the figures. They show a rather stark contrast between the first postwar decades and the period following the 1973 oil crisis. Thus, from 1946 right up to the early 1970s, growth was running as high as 10 percent a year. However, during the

1970s, it slipped to about 5 percent. And, during the 1980s, it dropped even further, hovering around 4 percent. This betrays a very striking deceleration of Japan's growth from quite phenomenal to rather unspectacular levels.

Not surprisingly, during the whole postwar period, Japan's growth greatly exceeded that of the U.S. which only averaged some 2 percent. The Europeans fared somewhat better, closer to 3 and 4 percent.[22] But the interesting thing is that, while they lagged hopelessly behind Japan in the initial phase, of late the difference has not been so great. Moreover, during the past few decades, other economies have emerged in East and Southeast Asia which continued achieving impressive growth rates, frequently well above 10 percent, such as Japan has not seen in years.

So, Japan was no longer a growth hero either.[23] Also, as with productivity, its economic record was quite spotty. Progress was most rapid in manufacturing, especially in capital and technology-intensive sectors like steel, automobiles, and electronics. It performed less well for other aspects of manufacturing, agriculture, construction and many services. For the latter, the U.S. and Europe actually looked better on the whole.

This is crucial for the 1990s because many of the branches which contributed most to the economy are now weakening and declining, such as textiles, shipbuilding and certain metals. Even steel has ceased expanding. Thus, future growth must come from high tech sectors like computers, semiconductors, and robotics or more futuristic areas like new materials, biotechnology, and aerospace.[24] But that will not be enough to stimulate a much larger economy. Something must also be done for construction, distribution, and services.

Oddly enough, while Japan's growth had been admirable in earlier years and quite acceptable more recently, it has not resulted in the sort of prosperity one might have expected and has traditionally been found in lesser countries. The Japanese are still working many more hours than Europeans or Americans, they live in rather mediocre housing in terribly crowded cities. They are not quite "workaholics" living in "rabbit hutches," but they are certainly not behaving like some of the world's richest citizens, which they are on paper.[25]

In short, as for productivity, the economic justification for admiring Japan's management system is somewhat flawed, particularly as concerns the unevenness of growth and inadequate quality of life. Nor is it entirely relevant since Japan's growth rates have fallen much closer to the norm for older industrial economies and substantially below that of the newly industrializing countries.

Expansion . . . At All Costs

In one other way, Japanese companies succeeded, some of them quite impressively. The primary interest in raising productivity and keeping factories humming was to expand production and, while so doing, boost market share. The result has been rather extraordinary. Japanese companies had almost collapsed by war's end, they were still rather puny and fragile during the 1960s, yet by the 1980s they were among the world's largest with operations around the globe.

When it comes to the creation of world-class players, the Japanese are a phenomenal success. They already have more members of the *Fortune* 500 leading foreign companies than everybody else put together. They also boast, among other things, five of the world's 10 biggest banks, five of the world's 10 largest steelmakers, three of the world's 10 biggest automakers, six of the world's 10 largest electronics firms, five of the world's 10 biggest fiber and textile companies, and so on.[26]

There was almost unheard-of growth for some of the older firms, the Mitsuis and Mitsubishis. And this was exceeded by newcomers, entrepreneurial companies like Honda, Sony, and Matsushita. This growth and market share would seem to justify the effort and show how accomplished Japanese managers are. But, it overlooks some things. Most obviously, not all companies succeeded in growing. Quite to the contrary, many of them shrank or disappeared. For example, there were once 97 motorcycle makers, now there are only four viable ones. There were once even more producers of zippers, now YKK rules the roost.

The more serious drawback is that for every company, including the winners, there was a price to be paid. Part of it was the financial burden of expanding and upgrading production. As noted, more often than elsewhere, the decision was made to put up a completely new plant instead of renovating an older one. This was often more costly and occasionally wasteful. The costs were only increased by the quest for larger scale. The Japanese built plants not only bigger than their existing plants but also larger than any competitors were planning. The assumption was that costs would be justified by lower unit prices, an assumption which only worked if you could sell everything you produced. Many makers were simply stuck with excess capacity.

Naturally, in these brand new plants, managers wanted the very best machinery and equipment—at just about any cost as it would be paid for with increased productivity per worker. But it was not enough to have new machinery when the factory opened, more was brought in all the time. With rapid technological innovation and the wish to have the very best, costs continued mounting. Thanks to *kaizen*, this was an endless process. Companies were continually adding new features, producing new models, creating whole new generations of the same article. This meant they had to retool more often. Meanwhile, they reduced the product cycle so much that new products were developed (and factories built) before the old ones had outlived their usefulness.

Obviously, this was the sort of approach adopted by managers more concerned with expansion than almost anything else. The sole exception was market share. The mightiest urge of all was to rise a notch in the ranking or, conversely, avoid losing market share and slipping. There was plenty of anecdotal evidence of this, including highly publicized targets of ambitious companies. Managers who increased market share were promoted; those who lost too much were demoted. Each year, specialized publications listed market share down to the nearest tenth of a percent and the media celebrated the winners and scorned the losers.[27] No wonder academic surveys found that Japanese managers cited increased market share as their top goal.[28]

The rationale behind market share has been thoroughly debated.[29] Larger market share usually brings a larger production scale, larger runs bring down unit costs, thus making it possible to undercut competitors. Larger market share provides a solid base for adding new articles in the same line, or branching into other sectors, or exporting abroad. In Japan, it also attracts better employees and adds to a company's prestige and political clout.

In response to the argument that it hurts profitability, supporters of market share point out that in some ways it can actually contribute. Lower unit costs permit higher margins (assuming you don't lower the price even more). Larger market share spreads overhead more widely (assuming the money is not used for further expansion). By selling more units, you can earn less per unit and still achieve a larger total (assuming you do have a reasonable margin).

These various responses make sense (assuming they are not invalidated by the suggested caveats). But they are nowhere near as persuasive as the ultimate rationale. If you do not pursue market share, you may well lose out to those who are seeking it aggressively. If you lose too much market share, you could eventually shrink to the extent that costs are burdensome and profits small. Indeed, you could completely disappear and there would be no profits at all.

It might also be mentioned that there is a valid rationale for profitability. Higher profits, among other things, make it possible to invest more in plant and equipment, dear to the Japanese manager's heart. A strong balance sheet attracts further outside money, from banks or shareholders, equally attractive. It permits the company to pay workers more, which they should appreciate and would add to morale. Among the workers are managers and executives who could get bigger perks. While less interesting, it is possible to pay more taxes which at least permits the government to build a better infrastructure and provide better services and welfare. In fact, there is even an ultimate rationale—if you don't make any profits and slip into debt you could disappear just as well.

The Japanese might mull over these benefits because, in practice and not in theory, they have been rather poor at generating profits. Profit levels are much lower in Japan than in the West or even in other parts of Asia. More worrisome is that there has not been any improvement in profitability over the years, despite slower expansion and more stress on the need for profits. Indeed, it should be noted, about half of Japan's companies show no profits at all!

Why have the Japanese done so poorly at profitability? One obvious reason is that they regard market share more highly and only vaguely realize the benefits of a sound bottom line. More serious is that no one in the company is pushing for it. Financial officers are few and weak and shareholders are usually passive. Top executives are mostly production or marketing types and not accountants (there are hardly any "bean counters" in Japan). Worse, praise and perks go to those who expand the company base, raise it in the market share ranking, and provide more jobs and promotion possibilities for the rest of the staff.

But the crucial explanation—and excuse—is that no company or executive can increase profitability alone. The shift from market share to profitability must be made by all together, otherwise those espousing market share will win out over those favoring profits. You simply cannot resist when a competitor suddenly expands scale, introduces new products or models, or lowers prices with the intention of gaining sales and market share. You never know how far this will go and just how much your market share may shrink if you do not react. The result is eternal suspicion and periodic bouts of competition. The worst are dubbed *kato kyoso* or "excessive competition" because they are a no-holds-barred struggle for market share, whatever the cost, whatever the impact on the bottom line.

Under these circumstances, Japanese managers cannot really afford to pursue profitability as eagerly as they otherwise might. Instead, they gloss over present performance with a reference to the company's goal of long-term gains and profits in due course. When those profits will come is uncertain, how big they will be is even less sure and whether they will justify the sacrifices undertaken until that day is sometimes questionable. In the meanwhile, Japanese managers get away with blunders for which any Western (or Asian) manager would be sacked. ■

Notes

1. See Benjamin Duke, *The Japanese School, Lessons for Industrial America*.

2. This section on *gambare*, draws on an interesting note by Dominique V. Turpin, "*Gambare*: Why Japanese Companies Won't Give Up," in *IMD Perspectives*, No. 3, 1991.

3. See Robert M. Marsh and Hiroshi Mannari, *Modernization and the Japanese Factory*.

4. For views on Japan's use of robots, written by a robotophile, see Frederick L. Schodt, *Inside The Robot Kingdom*.

5. See Toyota Motor Corp., *Toyota, A History of the First 50 Years*.

6. For case histories of assembler-supplier relations, see Smitka, *Competitive Ties*.

7. Hajime Ohta, "Productivity Growth in Japan—The Last Twenty Years," *United States-Japan Trade Council Report No. 39,* October 10, 1980.

8. See Walton, *The Deming Management Method.*

9. See Kaoru Ishikawa, *What Is Total Quality Control? The Japanese Way.*

10. See Japan Productivity Council, *Strategies for Productivity.*

11. See Masaaki Imai, *Kaizen, The Key to Japan's Competitive Success.*

12. For more on factory workers, see Cole, *Japanese Blue Collar,* and Arthur M. Whitehall and Shin-Ichi Takezawa, *The Other Worker.*

13. Ouchi, *Theory Z,* p. 79.

14. See Japan Human Relations Association, *Suggestions Activity Report,* Tokyo, annual.

15. This was shown most strikingly by Kamata, *Japan In The Passing Lane.*

16. Kamata, op. cit., p. 113.

17. For more on the role of labor unions, see Taishiro Shirai ed., *Contemporary Industrial Relations in Japan.*

18. See John W. Kendrick, "Explaining Differences in Productivity Trends Among OECD Countries," in *International Productivity Journal,* Winter 1991, pp. 85-90. Comparative statistics from OECD sources.

19. Japan Productivity Center, *Practical Handbook of Productivity and Labor Statistics,* Tokyo, annual.

20. See Chalmers, op. cit., and Smitka, op. cit.

21. JPC, *International Comparison of Productivity Level and Trends of Eleven OECD Countries*, 1989.

22. See World Bank, *World Development Report*, annual.

23. See William Emmott, *The Sun Also Sets*, and Jon Woronoff, *Japan: The (Coming) Economic Crisis*.

24. See Woronoff, *Japanese Targeting*.

25. See Woronoff, *Japan As—Anything But—Number One*.

26. Dodwell Marketing Consultants, *Industrial Groupings in Japan*, Tokyo, annual.

27. Yano Research Center, *Market Share in Japan*, Tokyo, annual.

28. See Ryuei Shimizu, "The Growth of Firms in Japan: An Empirical Study of Chief Executives," in Kazuo Sato and Yasuo Hoshino, *The Anatomy of Japanese Business*, p. 36.

29. One of the more interesting exchanges is that between Peter F. Drucker and Hugh Patrick, "Economic Realities and Enterprise Strategy," in Vogel ed., *Modern Japanese Organization and Decision-Making*, pp. 228-248.

3

Modern Factories, Backward Offices

Low-Productivity Administration

■ When a foreign visitor enters a modern Japanese factory, he is likely to gasp at what he sees. The factory itself is carefully designed, well arranged, and often attractive. The machinery is laid out in just the right place so that the flow of work will be smooth and continuous. The workers are stationed in the best position to use the machinery and to cooperate with one another. Their uniforms are spick and span and they are thoroughly absorbed in their work. Also in uniform, the foremen and supervisors, who know every aspect of operations, move about seeing that the work is done right and occasionally giving instructions. Then, after a long day's work, both senior operators and younger employees may stay on for a QC circle meeting to get their job done even better tomorrow.

When a foreign visitor enters a Japanese office, he is likely to gasp as well. This time it will be due to surprise and disappointment. In broad open spaces, with few partitions to provide the slightest privacy or even the possibility of concentration, there are masses of desks arranged seemingly every which way. Each cluster may represent a group or section with the respective supervisor at a desk on the end or a slight distance away. The desks of the employees will be facing one another and right next to each other so that they can consult . . . and also chat, it being rather hard to tell which is occurring. In a corner, there may be a partition with a table and some chairs where official guests can be received and served tea during a meeting. These places are usually full. And the atmosphere is so drab that often the employee takes his visitor out to a nearby coffee shop instead.

The desks are not tidy with everything in its place. Rather, papers and books are piled up helter skelter. If someone needs something he will go searching through the mass and perhaps end up not finding it there. These piles grow from day to day but rarely is an effort made to systematize them. And the standard office furnishings, including such common items as shelves and filing cabinets, are notably lacking. Forms are not much in use and messages are just jotted down on a handy scrap of paper. It frequently happens that someone has to leave his desk. But there may be no one in the room who knows just where he's gone or when he'll be back.

Working in this atmosphere are a variegated lot of employees. Some of the salarymen are impeccably dressed, others turn the office into a substitute living room or worse, drop their jackets and get into their slippers. Off to the side someone is making tea or perhaps even shaving. Only the young ladies are meticulous about their appearance, coming in the latest fashions and exquisitely made up for what, after all, is just a job. But, what is inside their heads is much more important than what they wear. And it could hardly be claimed that they are anywhere near as careful and meticulous about what they do and how they do it as the factory workers. Time is spent on essentials and inessentials indifferently, as things crop up. What cannot be done today will be continued after hours, or put off until the next day, or the day after.

That productivity is not a pressing matter is shown by the clear lack of the very things that symbolize it in the factory.[1] There are very few graphs of anything, aside perhaps from sales. Memos are rarely circulated to remind people of deadlines that must be met . . . and are sometimes missed. Basic records are scant. An employee will go about his daily work, meeting with suppliers or clients, discussing matters like prices and specifications, and finally reaching decisions that will bind the company and involve others in the implementation. Yet, he may just mention it to them in passing or bring it up in a meeting. Making him write it down would be an imposition. Thus, when a crucial person is absent or has been replaced, his successor may not know what to do.

When we consider the use of people, the contrast with the factory becomes particularly noticeable. Whereas every blue-collar worker is in his place, doing a specific job and one carefully designed to make the best use of him, it is often hard to know just what a white-collar employee is doing or supposed to do. Unlike Western companies, where the jobs are determined first and the employees hired to fill them, in Japan one recruits fresh batches of employees annually. They are differentiated by background, things like education and age, but rarely by specific job skills. Then they are sorted into categories, such as operational or clerical, also according to background. Finally, they are allocated to the sections and divisions that say they need more staff (or just want to grow) and any surplus seems to be dumped with sales, for the more sales personnel the better.

But there is no clearly defined job for them. "Job descriptions" do not exist in Japanese offices nor does the concept really exist in the Japanese mind.[2] Attempts at introducing job classifications have been strongly resisted so those assigned to a unit are usually left to sort out how the tasks they encounter will be shared. In some cases, each person may handle a given aspect. More often, the group will take it on as a group project. Obviously, many assignments can be accomplished either by individuals or a group. With a group, however, there is a greater probability that there will be either too few members, straining their capacity, or more likely yet, too many group members, meaning that some have little to do or all accomplish less than otherwise. How they tackle a given task is also left up to them more than in a Western enterprise—or a Japanese factory—where there are clear instructions as to how things should be done. They will receive advice from older employees and can check with their supervisor. In cases where there are no guidelines or precedents, they can initiate a *ringisho*. But it would be much simpler and more sensible if jobs were regarded as a valid concept.

The whole situation becomes even more fluid due to the considerable degree of rotation that occurs in any administration. Admittedly, in the factory, a lathe operator can be turned into a welder if needed. But, by and large, a person has a specific job which he keeps, in which he accumulates experience, and which he ends up knowing through and through. In offices, clerical staff, and especially potential managers, are kept on the move. They are sent from one section to the next every two or three years, sometimes they move after a single year. This makes it hard for them to gain more than a passing familiarity with the job and they are never as competent as Westerners trained and hired to do a specific job.

Supervisors, whether at section, division, or department level, also lack specific competences.[3] Unlike Western managers, they are not there to give orders and see that they are carried out. Unlike a Japanese foreman, they are not supposed to keep a constant check on how well subordinate staff are performing. In the office, they tend more to create an atmosphere in which everyone will do his best. Such an atmosphere involves leaving subordinates a considerable amount of leeway, guiding them on occasion, but never bearing down on them or making unpleasant criticism. The major tasks seem to be maintaining morale and arousing enthusiasm. Thus, the Japanese often compare this kind of manager to the leader of a group carrying the portable shrine (*mikoshi*) during festivals, giving directions and urging them on. Westerners might regard the manager as a mixture of coach and cheerleader.[4]

In such a situation, one cannot expect very high efficiency in the office or any degree of regularity in the way the company's affairs are handled. Too much is left to chance and to the personality of those involved. There is a saving grace in the sense that, once given their head and aroused to a high enough pitch, the Japanese will make every effort to fulfill the trust placed in them. But it is extremely hard to maintain a fevered pitch of enthusiasm and perhaps dangerous to act in such an exalted state constantly. Companies are rather humdrum affairs once they have been run in. The brilliant campaigns and actions that were appropriate while Japan's economy was growing rapidly could be counterproductive today.

The disadvantages of the Japanese approach should also not be obscured by the well-known fact that the Japanese work very long hours and are willing to put in overtime (which leads some foreigners to assume that they work "hard"). Much of this is pointless since, in all too many cases, the Japanese employees accomplish no more than they could have, or many Western employees do, in much fewer hours by working in a more concentrated and rational fashion. Their efficiency could be increased vastly by a few appropriate measures and probably doubled by a systematic revision.

More important than method is substance. And it is worrisome that the primary purpose of administrative offices seem to get short shrift. The factory is expected to produce, but it is the office that must keep very careful track of production costs. During much of the period of rapid growth, the main concern was to get enough raw materials from the suppliers at whatever price. Now price has to be scrutinized more minutely. Increasingly, the amount of raw materials and energy used is controlled. But the office keeps much poorer records of other costs, especially for functions accomplished in-house, whether this is sales, transport, or advertising. With a staff of a given size, which has to be used one way or the other, it apparently does not make much sense to check whether each staff member is really carrying his weight in financial terms.

If the factory is to produce, then certainly the office must decide how much to produce as a function of potential sales. It is very risky to expand production facilities without having a good idea of who will buy the products. Yet, market forecasting is still backward and many essential decisions, involving tremendous amounts of money that will be immobilized for extended periods of time, result from rather extraneous factors. Expansion will occur if the man in charge is dynamic, or if there are excess funds available, or in order to keep up with the competitors. The urge for market share has encouraged many ill-conceived investments and resulted in overcapacity and overproduction. Japanese managers may deny these flaws. But, how else can one explain the repeated bursts of expansion, followed by price wars, followed by the freezing and finally scrapping of plant in a whole string of industries, from textiles and shipbuilding to steel, and now even electronics and semiconductors.

The art of proper management, as many Japanese managers have yet to learn, is the art of balance. There is no point to increasing productive capacity unless one is pretty certain of sales. Otherwise, the company will work under capacity or produce too much and have to sell at a low price. This the Japanese try to avoid by turning sales into a campaign just as expanding production had been. Sales, however, is a costly operation since it employs large numbers of personnel. And once it becomes a serious campaign the chance that the salesmen will get good prices for their products is smaller than ever. Finally, no matter how important production or sales may be, nothing exceeds the significance of keeping a healthy balance between receipts and expenditures. No conceivable amount of future benefits (often quite dimly seen) should blind a manager to the dangers of a cash flow squeeze.

These are not minor problems by any means. From top to bottom, measures could be taken that would make better use of personnel or permit a company to use less personnel to accomplish as much. The savings are not just a few yen here and there but very substantial amounts that would accrue over the long term. In more serious cases, failing to abide by what is standard managerial practice elsewhere can even place the company in jeopardy. Of course, the Japanese frequently admit the weaknesses of their system and on occasion modest reforms are actually introduced. But so far productivity has made little headway at the administrative and management level. It has run into too solid resistance rooted not in any objective view of the situation, but subjective preferences and time-honored traditions.

No Time to Work

People, we all know, are the most crucial element in any company, bureaucracy, or social institution. Without their cooperation nothing can be accomplished and they must be treated properly to enhance participation. The greatest care must be shown in relating to staff and staffers must feel that they enjoy respect. Yet, paradoxically, because people are so important in Japan they are often wasted and even squandered outrageously. They can end up accomplishing much less than people in other countries where their worth is not acknowledged and they are treated more impersonally.

Nowhere is this clearer than when it comes to Japanese-style decision-making. This involves various methods that are too well known to bother describing in much detail. There is *ringi seido*, a consultation system which theoretically at least starts at the bottom, with a proposal (*ringisho*) working its way upward for approval or sanction (*kessai*). There is *nemawashi*, where informal approaches are made to gain support of a given action and may result in an informal meeting (*kondankai*) or a more formal conference to consider implementation (*kaigi*). But there is not—in theory at least—a situation in which one person or a small group can make basic decisions for the whole company.

There are many advantages to the Japanese form of decision-making.[5] It provides for some degree of democracy and spontaneity in that staff at lower levels can initiate measures, or work out plans, or make proposals which will be channeled upward to higher levels. It also provides for greater participation, especially when combined with meetings, since all those even remotely involved in an issue will be invited to attend and present their views. They will also hear the views of the other parties. This having been done, a decision adopted on the basis of consensus, or so it is claimed, will meet with general acceptance. This reinforces harmony within the company and should encourage all to give their unstinting support to implementation of new measures.

Still, admitting the advantages is no reason to overlook the drawbacks. Some of them are minor and tolerable, others are essential and can cause considerable problems. Most of them are known to Japanese managers, some of whom are quite annoyed by the defects. Those which are of greatest interest here are the ones that encourage a poor use of personnel.

The first demerit is that there are too many people involved. A *ringisho*, which may actually only concern one section and quite a minor matter, may well end up being sent to various other sections and collecting an incredible number of seals before it gets back to its originator. Meetings tend to expand, as more people are invited, whether or not directly involved. In fact, when in doubt a person is more likely to be invited than left out ... just in case. There is no desire to slight those who will feel they are being ignored although, once asked to come, they may discover that they are wasting their time. Worse, by coming and raising unnecessary questions or making proposals concerning matters that do not really concern them, they will be wasting everyone else's time as well.

This sort of exercise occurs all too frequently. There are many important and valid reasons for holding meetings. Members of different sections and divisions must cooperate, coordination is necessary between the various members of a group, contacts have to be maintained with suppliers and clients. But meetings are also held for minor things, requesting a favor that is easier to ask in person or, worse, holding meetings or seeing people just because the more personal contacts there are the smoother things should run even if there is no specific purpose. And one meeting always seems to call for another. Thus, according to the Japan Management Association, managers were spending fully 40 percent of their time on meetings and conferences.[6]

Too many people attending too many meetings is obviously compounded if the meetings are also too long. This they will certainly be if more, rather than fewer, participants attend. But they will also be longer because of the Japanese approach to decision-making. Rather than come right out with a proposal, debate it, and approve or reject it, one must go through all the proper motions. The participants, to avoid upsetting one another, will only make their proposals slowly and cautiously, waiting for signs of approval, before proceeding further. Any opponents will be just as cautious, not wishing to make enemies unnecessarily. And, if it is impossible for a decision to be reached at the first meeting, there will be a second, and a third, and more.

The Japanese seem to think that the loss of time doesn't really matter as long as one ends up with a good decision. But they are very wrong. First of all, there is the fact that time does mean money. Although frequently ignored by Japanese companies, now that wages are so high, time ill spent can cost extraordinary sums. Secondly, there is no reason to believe that a decision that has taken a longer time to mature is inherently that much better. But, the biggest problem is that while the decision is being forged there can be no action. Whatever inappropriate methods called for a *ringisho* will continue until it is approved. If a decision is necessary to implement a plan, that plan will have to wait.

Sometimes it may not matter; other times the decision may simply come too late. It is, of course, easy to tell when a hasty decision has led to damage or loss for the company. A tardy decision can have equally bad effects, even if they are hard to see or judge. Thus, for example, if a foreign buyer gets tired of waiting for a decision and lets another Japanese or more likely Korean or Taiwanese company clinch the deal, the loss of earnings will not be visible but it will be real. When, in a particularly decisive case, Sumitomo Shoji was too slow in making up its mind, it lost the remnants of Ataka to its rival, C. Itoh. This is just one case among countless others.

Alongside the quantitative factors, there is also a qualitative one. Since great efforts were made at being cooperative and preserving harmony, one could hardly say that everything was clearly expressed. People who were against a measure, noting they were in a minority, may well have kept their views to themselves. There is usually also an effort to keep decisions as flexible and open to change as possible. All this combines to make many agreements sufficiently vague that they can be implemented differently by the various parties with each claiming it has followed the consensus. If the decision was never written down, as frequently happens, it would be impossible to prove who really was right.

But the biggest flaw lies elsewhere. To some extent the decision-making process is just for show. It is not a spontaneous coming together in which ideas can proceed from the bottom upward. No matter how diffuse they may seem, there is always an originator, someone who writes the *ringisho* or someone who starts convincing the others of his own view in *nemawashi*. The meetings convened are only ceremonial . . . unless there is strong resistance from another party. The final decision, however, will result from the basic power relationship between the participants. Although lower ranking staff are also invited, they know better than to sponsor proposals without backing from higher up. So the decisions will rarely be imposed by those below. That being so, why go through all the rituals and formalities when everyone knows they are a sham?

Harmony and Loyalty First!

Japanese companies are often more like social organisms than commercial enterprises especially because of the strong emphasis placed on the type of person wanted rather than his abilities. Personality plays an exceptional role in determining who is recruited, how one behaves, and who gets promoted. Among the characteristics most praised, none are evaluated more highly than harmony (*wa*) and loyalty (*chusei-shin*).[7] They are enshrined in the slogans and mottos of the corporation and placed, sometimes in delicate calligraphy, in prominent locations. They crop up in every speech by executives, from the chairman on down.[8]

Candidates for recruitment know that, whether true to their nature or not, they have to appear as tame and responsive as possible and emphasize their willingness to serve the company in any way it desires. They should not have any strong attachments or family obligations that could lessen their commitment. Although they can have their own ideas and hobbies, this should not get in the way of serving the company. The company personnel officers meanwhile are looking for likeable young people who can be molded later to fit the company's needs. This is admitted by any number of senior staff who refer to the ideal young recruit as a "blank sheet of paper."

True, Mitsui likes slightly aggressive types, while Mitsubishi is more on the conservative side. Toshiba-men are rather drab while Sony's staff are more flamboyant. And there are fashions when the corporate world claims it is seeking self-confident, dynamic or daring employees. This is duly noted by the university grads who then show up for interviews prepared to go through that act. But the basic fact remains that, to get and keep a job, most Japanese are willing to alter or hide their true feelings and adopt the outer shell their employer wants. One must give up one's "self" on entering the company.

It is not enough just to find people who "fit" the company image. Once within, they must become a different kind of person. This process begins with the initiation ceremony and carries over to a training process that places more emphasis than elsewhere on the spiritual side. More extreme cases include "work-begging" or camps that include marathons, self-criticism, and zen. Even the Self-Defense Force lends a hand to train tough salarymen. Throughout, the emphasis is on duty, obedience, loyalty, and harmony.

Over the following years the salaryman gets to know his colleagues, with some of whom he will spend his whole career. Slowly but surely, he works his way through the company, transferred to this division and that, sent off to distant subsidiaries and overseas offices. Gradually, he becomes part of a growing circle of company people and his style adapts to theirs. He meets his colleagues not only during working hours, but at lunch in the company canteen or a nearby restaurant, after work for a drink, or during a night on the town. He may go on company trips, attend company social activities, and belong to a company club or sports team. As if that were not enough, many employees also live in company housing.

Such constant contact with other company people helps create a spirit of teamwork that can hardly be replicated elsewhere. But it is apparently not quite enough for the company, for any rough edges must be smoothed. It is not good enough to be a team member, one must merge with the team. Standing out and being noticed in teamwork is almost as bad as not participating and is more likely to show wrong attitude than mark one for later promotion as having more initiative or dynamism.

The experience of working together rounds off other rough edges. One will not get very far in the company without a fair number of friends. The easiest way to win and hold them is to be as understanding and accepting as possible. Even at meetings which are supposedly called to obtain people's reactions, it would be extremely foolish to say anything that might be taken as criticism or just a slight on someone else. Naturally, one should say and do nothing that might lead people to suspect that any self-flattery was intended or that there was an undue sign of ambition. No matter how badly a promotion is desired, the best thing is to wait and be discovered. Drawing attention to oneself only arouses jealousy and antagonism.

Thus, even the most spirited and recalcitrant subject can, over the years, be turned into a model company man. We have all seen freshman employees who undergo a complete conversion. Only a few years before they were insisting they would never join the rat race, and now it's everything for the company. It is quite possible that the same process will continue even with the less than ideal material of the present younger generation. But it is bound to be harder to convince them and there will be a growing segment who refuse to give up all their outside interests. There will be more and more who quite simply refuse to enter companies whose demands are too stringent.

Although harmony is an admirable trait, it does have drawbacks, and they are particularly serious when the drive for harmony is pushed this far. One problem is the lack of an objective yardstick for evaluating the success of policy. Another is the difficulty in having a sufficiently detached attitude to attempt evaluation. When everyone is on the same team, it is very hard for a member to judge the whole team. When anything resembling criticism of the team or its members is regarded as disturbing harmony, it is quite impossible to admit failings, seek the causes, and make changes.

In fact, the relations are such that the very idea of objectivity is not quite in its place. Like the wartime leaders, Japanese managers make appeals to the spirit of their subordinates. They try to arouse a passionate loyalty, a keen urge to win, a tenaciousness in attaining goals . . . but never an attempt to question the goals or purposes. No appeal is made to the mind to stop, consider attentively, and then systematically judge both what is right and wrong in a given policy. That is why it so often happens that Japanese companies, once having come to a decision, will follow through ruthlessly whatever the results may be. If the decision was wise, harmony is a plus; if the decision was mistaken, harmony can be utterly destructive.

Without wishing to be heretical, it must be admitted that there are some things for which teamwork is not particularly suitable. The group approach is admirable for assembly line work, excellent to keep up morale in the office, and can arouse greater efforts in sales. Teamwork is supposedly an asset in research and development. But making the team a must often means that more people than necessary are assigned to a given project. There are many things that can be done just as well, or almost as well, by individuals or a few people. This involves a definite savings in personnel expenses that can no longer be ignored. More crucially, there are things of a creative nature which can only be done well by individuals. Most truly great ideas can be traced back to one person who would have performed less well in the stultifying atmosphere of Japanese teams. That is why imagination and creativity are so obviously lacking. And officially adopting slogans like "be imaginative" and "be creative" will not help.

Loyalty is also a fine virtue. But it has its drawbacks, too. One has already been referred to, the willingness to blindly accept something because it is suggested by one's superior or imposed for the good of the company. This weakens the critical faculty that every businessman (and every human being) should preserve. Another is that such loyalty discourages all of the virtues that are associated with leadership. Throughout a person's early career, his advancement depends on his ability to follow orders whether they appeal to him or not. His opinion is asked, but it is the foolhardy salaryman who would contradict his boss or suggest an alternative without great diplomacy. Not until one enters middle management can one act as a leader. For reasons of harmony, however, this type of leadership is to look after one's subordinates or raise their morale. So, only on entering top management, after nearly three decades of taking orders, does one finally give orders and show true leadership.

Loyalty makes the crisis more serious, for Japanese leaders almost systematically seek out weak and compliant successors. Even founders of great companies, those who showed their personal ability, like Konosuke Matsushita and Soichiro Honda, preferred less dynamic subordinates, those who lack "self."[9] Further on down, each new class of freshman employees is taught about loyalty and expected to follow the path indicated to them. We have now gone through over forty entry classes since the war. Just about everyone on the spiral staircase has been thoroughly drilled in all matters of harmony and loyalty. Will they still be able to direct their companies and the economy when they reach the top?

Keeping Up Human Relations

Ever since Meiji days, businessmen have compared the company to the family, more exactly, to the tight-knit and strictly disciplined Japanese family. There were periods in which familism became the predominant philosophy of Japanese business leaders and ultimately the official ideology of the state. Of course, those insisting that the company was a family were not just being sentimental. They had their own reasons. They wished to foster dedication and hard work, they wanted to hold on to their personnel, and they wished to direct things as freely and unrestrictedly as possible.

Familism collapsed after the war. In fact, the traditional Japanese family has undergone such drastic changes that it might not really serve very well as the basis for a company structure. But the Japanese have not been able to throw off their attachment to close social relations that often influence, and sometimes even dominate, purely commercial matters. In many ways, the Japanese company is a social unit just as much as an economic unit. And the action of management and labor can never be grasped without taking the social arrangements into account.

In order to hold on to its staff, the company offers many benefits that are not readily available elsewhere. Over and above the wages, the company often provides dormitories or housing, medical care, perhaps its own doctor and clinic. It promises a welcome retirement payment or pension after the career with the company is over and sometimes also a second job. It subsidizes meals in the company canteen and pays for travel expenses to work. It often goes so far as to provide sports grounds, club rooms, and vacation homes. The frills vary with the size and wealth of the company, but there are always special advantages that make the employees depend more heavily on the employer.

Not only are there material facilities of this sort, the company also takes an active interest in the life of its employees. From the very start, the personnel division carefully looks into the family background and personality of prospective employees. It informs them of their duties and sees to it that they accept their responsibilities. On the other hand, it also shows unusual interest in how the employee is doing. Any sign that a person is poorly accepted or discontented will be noted. If there are personal problems that can be solved, assistance will be offered. In short, it pries into the employee's personal life to an extent that would hardly be accepted elsewhere but seems quite normal in Japan.[10]

Going considerably further, the personnel division carefully organizes the original training and initiation sessions when the new staff is welcomed into the company. It follows up by seeing that the new personnel is well integrated in their sections. Outside of work, there may be lessons, classes, parties, trips and the like to allow staff members to meet one another. Some companies even go so far as to have their own clubs to encourage matrimony and many a manager would propose a potential spouse and appear at the wedding as the go-between.

The foreman or supervisor also does his bit. He shares most of the work activities with his subordinates and eats in the same canteen. He is encouraged to be as friendly as possible and is evaluated by his ability to get along with, as opposed to directing or ordering about, his subordinates. He may take this a step further and join them periodically in their drinking bouts outside work. Having created this rapport, he is repaid with trust. His subordinates will work harder and show greater loyalty so that he looks better in the eyes of higher management. In return, he is expected to prevail in their favor if there is trouble.[11]

Among the white-collar workers, the section chief or *kacho* performs much the same tasks. He is not meant to be a supervisor in the sense of keeping a sharp eye out for mistakes. Rather, he offers a presence so that when his subordinates are in need of advice or think they have made a mistake, they can come to him. Even if they make foolish errors, he would tend not to criticize too harshly for fear of destroying the rapport he has striven so hard to create. Instead, he may just chide them or actually assume the responsibility. In addition to this, our poor *kacho* has to spend countless hours drinking with his staff to get to know their innermost feelings.

Finally, the president and top directors, aside from their normal tasks in running the company, have a whole array of ceremonial tasks which keep them busy making speeches, officiating at meetings, attending receptions, and so on. They must also appear as peace-makers if there are disputes among the lower level managers or help smooth over differences between sections and divisions. Indeed, at this level the social tasks are often so numerous that there is hardly any time left over for managing.

The web of social relationships, already quite dense by non-Japanese standards, spreads yet further. There are many informal relations that are equally important. Some of them are between employees of the same entry year. The men will tend to go out for a drink after work, the women perhaps for a coffee and cake. Those who studied at the same university, or worked together at the same overseas office, will also meet periodically. Many younger employees enter friendly links with older colleagues which, over the years, solidify into *oyabun-kobun* (mentor-follower) relations. Through these various networks, they will occasionally become part of broader cliques.

Those in managerial positions will have further social demands placed on them by the need for good human relations (*ningen kankei*). Contacts with other managers, either on the same level or higher up, must be maintained formally as well as informally. Anyone dealing with either clients or suppliers cannot avoid getting to know them personally for the greater good of their mutual relations. This entails a meal or an evening out for drinks. Just how far this custom goes is shown by repeated polls where many young salarymen entertain or meet colleagues at least once a week while some older ones almost never get home before midnight.

There is no doubt that such activities are extremely fruitful. They contribute to more harmonious relations between staff members at high or low levels. They oil the social relations that make business flow more smoothly. They create an essential rapport among those responsible for getting things done. In the context of lifetime employment, they are even more crucial than otherwise. For, working together a good 20 or 30 years, employees are more seriously in need of good friendly relations than if they were only dealing with one another briefly or less directly.

Nevertheless, just as for everything else in business, keeping up human relations has a price. There are valid reasons to believe that this price is exceedingly high.

First come the direct costs. The various aspects of corporate welfare are not inexpensive. Most companies offer an impressive array of allowances from commuting and dangerous work to postings in remote areas. They are bound to provide pensions, social security, and medical care, and sometimes offer more than is legally required. Frills like company picnics, company trips, and company parties add up. If they also provide subsidized housing or housing loans, the burden becomes heavier. It all comes to about 16 percent of labor costs, roughly split between the statutory and non-statutory (or voluntary) welfare expenses.[12]

In addition to this, there is the far from minor cost of entertainment offered clients and suppliers. Given the many pretexts for such activities, this also mounts quite rapidly. In fact, in 1989, the total spent on business entertainment reached nearly ¥5 trillion. This represented about ¥4.2 for each ¥1,000 of sales and amounted to a massive flow of nearly ¥14 billion a day spent on wining and dining at a time when more than half the companies were making losses rather than profits. This one item was roughly the size of company R&D, or the government's education budget.

No less important, these activities are tremendously time-consuming in that any number of people, not only in the personnel and sales divisions but throughout the hierarchy, have to take it upon themselves to create better relations. Since it is harder to pry open the shell of most Japanese, the time consumed is greater than in other societies. Since it takes a long time for business relationships to mature, and it is essential to keep them cordial, the entertainment stints have to be relatively frequent. It is not only the direct costs but the time spent by staff in keeping up human relations that must be evaluated either in terms of extra wages or other uses. On this basis, the price may be staggering.

Obviously, since growth slowed down, companies are more concerned about reducing costs and they increasingly wonder whether these particular costs are not too high. An added reason for doubt is that the companies seem to be getting less back for their investment than ever. After all, the purpose of company welfare and entertainment is not just to spread good will but to keep the personnel working diligently and showing loyalty. Meanwhile, what was once a gift has often turned into a right. Workers now regard welfare facilities as their due and even bonuses, once given out at option by the company, have become regular payments which are painfully negotiated each year.

Despite everything they give, and although morale is still high by international standards, Japanese companies are certainly not getting the same old dedication. No matter what they do they cannot convince the new classes of salarymen to relinquish all their other concerns and interests. That is because, with a different upbringing and life style, many younger employees feel that they are not getting what they want either. The price for surrendering their "self" to the company is too high when what they want most is to get back home, see their family, or engage in sports and leisure.

Thus, the old social contract between management and labor, the contract that has never been written down but is almost as important as the employment contract, may be seriously altered in the future. The company will count what it gives more stingily just as its employees begrudge the time and emotion they have to invest. Increasingly Japan will become a society in which people work for a salary and expect their rewards in material rather than moral form.

The Bureaucracy-Man

Although the term "salaryman" is derived from English, in practice the Japanese *sarariman* hardly compares with an office worker, middle manager or other employee in the Western world. The model for the Japanese management system, despite any superficial resemblance, does not seem to be that of Western management. Actually, the salaryman barely even resembles a businessman, whether an entrepreneur or less dynamic type. Looking for Japanese parallels is also confusing. The basic inspiration does not appear to be the Edo merchant, nor the rich landowner, nor the *samurai*. If anything, it is the bureaucrat.

The salaryman is recruited much like a bureaucrat.[16] He is not hired for a specific job but membership in a given group. New entrants are taken in once a year at the bottom. What is sought is more the generalist than the specialist and more stress is placed on loyalty than ability. Thus, the tests to screen new entrants examines some general knowledge and then, in more detail, personality to see how one's character fits in with the prevailing mentality. Attention is paid to the schools one attended, one's family background, and, increasingly, character references from sponsors or other connections.

The process is very similar to the choice of Japanese bureaucrats for the civil service. Many of the same people who end up in a Japanese business concern might just as well have entered a government department. In fact, many of the college graduates, and increasingly high school grads as well, apply both for jobs in government and business, indifferently. The earlier preference for business, with its possibilities of rising to the top, is now succumbing to interest in government, where one's career is calmer and more secure. Thus, a tendency to adopt a bureaucratic mentality is spreading even among young people from whom one might have expected more ambition.

Once within a company, promotion is gradual, one step at a time, just like a bureaucrat. One reaches managerial positions not through clear signs of talent but by slow movement up a spiral staircase. True, more clever or dynamic individuals may arrive a bit earlier, but only a wee bit. And they arouse enmity among those they pass. Ambition is not really rewarded by the system and it is penalized by all those who fear they cannot do as well. Thus, every effort so far to introduce merit ratings, evaluations of work, or even job descriptions that would single out individuals and make it possible to see how well they perform, as opposed to others, has been sabotaged. Seniority, although not fully approved of, is accepted as the safer and "more objective" means of promotion.

Of course, some people do make it to the top and others get stuck further down. Doubtlessly, those who show greater ability will have an advantage. But this is balanced by another bureaucratic trait, namely the role of personal connections. They often arise out of the job rotation system, a method rarely followed by commercial enterprises elsewhere. Over the years, the salaryman is shifted from office to office, job to job, and gets to know the company as a business. He also gets to know the people who make up the company and establishes personal relations with them. He creates a network of relationships that will ultimately help him and in the meanwhile aid those above him, his friends and sponsors, his *sempai* (seniors) or *oyabun* (patrons), to rise. The guiding principle thus becomes not what you know but who you know.

The fact that a person's career occurs within the same company and that one is constantly dealing with the same people means that personal relations and subjective reactions frequently gain precedence over more impersonal and objective concerns. As long as an issue is relatively straightforward, where to place a machine, how to use it, or the like, there is little trouble. But almost all issues also have consequences for the people involved. Thus, for example, it might be harder to decide on investment, expansion, retrenchment, or, especially, personnel and promotion issues, because any decision is likely to raise or lower the status of those concerned. The hardest point is to admit the failure of past policy and especially to pin the blame for having introduced an unsuccessful measure.

Despite the breath of democratization after the war, a bureaucratic system like Japan's does not take long to replace the old order with a new ranking. Thus, there are clear distinctions once again between white-collar and blue-collar, between men and women, between those with or without titles. The competition for a title, any title, has become so intense that many companies have to grant titles when employees reach a certain level (or just age) although they are not accompanied by an increase in responsibility and sometimes even salary. Yet, to forget one's position would be very dangerous. It is necessary for subordinates to address superiors correctly, using the proper polite language, and occasionally to make a modest bow. Even the petty distinctions between those who entered a year earlier or a year later, who is called *san* and who *kun,* have not disappeared at the bottom. Meanwhile, at the top, the bowing and scraping is tremendous, a grotesque reminder of the days when the elite bureaucrats were also high ranking *samurai.*

It is not that the basic motive is bad. Every company, factory, or store can do with a degree of institutionalization. For any human organism to run smoothly, it is necessary to work out the best ways of doing things and then see to it that these ways are maintained. It is useful to lay down routines and procedures and keep them going. Rules and regulations have to be established and passed down so that one knows how to act in a given situation. But there must always be some flexibility so as to introduce changes when appropriate. And decisions once taken must not continue perpetually without carefully checking that the circumstances have not changed.

Unfortunately, Japan tends to be an unusually conservative society. It is extremely difficult to come to decisions or to create precedents. Once that is done, however, it is well near impossible to change them unless there are very compelling reasons. The first thing one does when an issue arises is not even to judge it on its own merits but to check the precedents. The most common reason for rejecting a proposal or request is quite simply ". . . since there are no precedents (*zenrei*)." In the world of business, however, things are always occurring for which there are no precedents although a bureaucracy dislikes such repeated challenges.

Going by the rules is fine. But a rule tends to bind a person even more when he is also encouraged to maintain harmony or follow tradition rather than show imagination or seize initiative. Thus, Japanese companies—like Japanese bureaucracies—tend to get bogged down under a mountain of precedents and rules that may no longer apply. And the method of reversing them is equally slow and bureaucratic: *ringisho* and meetings.

A bureaucratic approach can be very expensive as well. With the need to appear solid or powerful, staffs expand beyond normal needs and office space, let alone facade and decoration, are sometimes excessive. With a clear hierarchy geared not only to production or sales but to keeping up appearances and assuming status, it is too easy to give in to empire-building. We all know of companies that have set up subsidiaries locally or opened offices abroad just to keep up with the competitors. What is worse, many have done so just because they had the staff on the payroll and did not know what to do with them. And sometimes a subsidiary was created simply so that those in power would have a place to retire. For such reasons, Japan falls victim to all of Parkinson's laws with an exceptional facility.

Living within their own closed circle, namely a company whose members have largely been trained there and rarely worked anywhere else, Japanese salarymen tend to have a very limited horizon. They do not really know how things are done in other companies, aside from bits of gossip or short articles in the press. They know even less about how things are really done abroad. Thus, as Gojiro Hata, President of ECI, pointed out, the Japanese not only lack internationality, they also lack "intercompaniality."[13] That means that all they know is what is happening within their own company and their main advantage, as an executive, is to be able to react well there. But the abilities they show there may be worthless elsewhere. And certainly their most important asset, a solid network of intracompany connections, cannot be transferred.

This creates serious problems for their companies. Working together so long, the bureaucracy-men tend to think alike and act alike. Even if they hold radically different views, they hesitate to admit it. This is an excellent breeding ground for stereotyped reactions and group think. It is very dangerous when the range of options is cut down to this extent. A company in trouble would hardly know where to find advice or even fresh ideas. There is little intake of older staff. Advisors are not really welcome. And business consultants have general solutions while companies are very specific. So, many companies continue struggling with their problems—some do not even realize that any exist—until they solve them by trial and error or the situation becomes so bad that they succumb.

Bureaucracy stifles initiative within the company. But it also spreads throughout the economy. When companies form groups and associations to defend their interests, they may surreptitiously smother competition. Lack of competition can harm the consumer. But it can undermine the economy in an even more decisive manner. It can snuff out the spark that led entrepreneurs not so long ago to launch new ventures that have since proven their validity. Only because the industrial structure was still loose and there was room for new companies, could entrepreneurs like Soichiro Honda, Konosuke Matsushita, Akio Morita, and many more rise.[14] Only because the distribution system had to be reconstructed could it be altered by people like Isao Nakauchi, Seiji Tsutsumi, and Noboru Goto.

Now, however, things have settled considerably. Japan once again has its groups and quasi-*zaibatsu*, oligopolistic companies dominate most major fields, and distributors control the market by regulating the outlets. Government bureaucrats join together with company bureaucrats to encourage a more "stable" economy whereby there is an orderly growth or decrease in production and sales among those concerned. But there is no thought to the companies that do not yet exist or are too small to make their interests known. Japan, Inc. has always united the bureaucrats, but it was usually spurned by the most dynamic entrepreneurs. Now there is reason to wonder how many such entrepreneurs will see the light of day.

Thus, the spread of the bureaucratic mentality can be one of the gravest threats to Japan's economy. There is no reason to believe that bureaucratic modes are any good for business. Since one must constantly adapt to the market situation, try to match supply and demand, seek sales wherever they are available, keep up with technology, and also introduce innovations, business is—or should be—a very lively field. The businessman's strong point is not solidity or stability but the ability to adapt and change. Yet, that is becoming ever rarer in Japan.

Wasting Women Workers

Up until now, almost implicitly, we have been describing the workings of the Japanese management system as it applies to men. When it comes to women, the situation is quite different. The vast majority do not benefit from lifetime employment or anything like it, they do not enjoy an escalator ride to better jobs and higher wages, they do not get many of the welfare frills and the labor unions do not even pay much attention to their fate.

"Lifetime" employment was rarely an option for women. To start with, only regular workers in large companies were offered this while a disproportionate number of women worked for small companies or, even when employed by large companies, were not given regular status. Many were part-time workers, although this often involved more than forty hours a week. Others were ordinary temps or engaged in *arubaito*, the Japanese equivalent thereof. A large contingent worked at home.[15]

But even those who might have qualified for extended employment were pushed out of the workforce at a fairly young age. The employment curve for women assumed a very clear M-shape, with substantial numbers working from the age of 18 to 23 and then withdrawing to get married, have children, and raise a family. If they did not do so voluntarily, social pressure and corporate nastiness were used to get them out. When they reached their thirties and forties, however, many of these women returned to the labor force for a second stint. The reason was sometimes to broaden their horizon or occupy their free time, but increasingly it was to make ends meet.

As for the career escalator, fewer women got on and it carried those who did less far. As noted, many retired in their twenties and thereby forfeited the advantages of seniority. Even the fact that they might leave was used against younger employees to keep them from entering more promising career paths. This occurred despite a highly touted Equal Employment Opportunity Law, adopted in 1986 more under international pressure than from Japan's own volition.[16]

The failure of this legislation is easy to understand. For one, it only required voluntary compliance and any company which did not wish to apply the new rules could just ignore them, since there were no penalties. The other explanation is that companies moved from open sex discrimination to using more veiled tactics. The key to this was a dual track system under which new recruits were offered the choice between *sogo shoku* or "comprehensive work" and *ippan shoku* or "general work." The former involved extensive training and advancement opportunities and the latter less promotion and lower wages. To join the former, however, women had to accept long hours, short vacations and, above all, the company's right to relocate them wherever and whenever it wanted. It was usually that last requirement which women could not accept.

Whatever the reasons, the outcome was that most women ended up with "general work" while the bulk of the men enlisted for "comprehensive work." Thus, they were on two very different escalators. While the men's escalator rose steadily, the women's remained fairly flat. The consequence was that rather few women obtained promotions and those who did had to wait longer. In addition, women were usually only promoted to positions where they supervised other women. Token numbers made it to section head while hardly any ever became senior executives.

The situation was no better for wages. Even when recruited into the same companies, women were often given lesser positions which earned somewhat lower salaries. This small initial gap only continued growing over the years, showing a pronounced disparity as women resigned to raise a family and hardly improving when they returned to the labor force. The second time around, they usually had even worse jobs with lower pay than the first time. On the whole, the average female wage was only 60 percent of the average male wage. That was the lowest level for an

OECD country and Japan was the only one where the gap actually grew.[17]

This discrimination became ever less tolerable for women, but there was little they could do to avoid it. Not surprisingly, they were far from "happy" workers. A cross-country survey of Japan, Australia, Brazil, Germany, and the U.S. showed that Japanese women were the most dissatisfied with their jobs. One out of three complained of long hours, low wages, and poor interpersonal relations while only about one in six of the others did so.

It is obvious that, if women were dissatisfied, they would not perform as well. That had been conceded by men, and all sorts of techniques were adopted to boost morale. Women had naturally been included in the QC Circles and productivity drives and, on the whole, they were put to good use in the factories. It was in the offices that Japanese management again failed, this time quite miserably.

Most office employees were college graduates and, in many cases, female recruits were as well-educated as men. Some also possessed greater imagination and creativity. But they were usually not allowed to display this. Even if on the fast track, they suffered from handicaps against men since socializing is so important. Married women and those who had families, especially, were strapped for time and under great strain. However, the big question seemed to be what to do with the "general" workers who were not expected to stay long with the company and were therefore not trained or given positions of responsibility.

The solution which evolved over the past few decades has been to employ them in the rather odd function of "office lady." These OLs, as they are called, were simply expected to keep busy around the office, doing whatever was necessary. They could not even be regarded as proper assistants to male colleagues in most cases since they were just used to take phone calls, do some filing, or deliver messages. In earlier days, they also typed out handwritten notes for their superiors. Now, the typing pool has been turned into a computer pool, so they key in material their male colleagues are too lazy to do themselves. Finally, in almost all cases, women are used to serve tea.[18]

It is hard to imagine just how wasteful the career of an office lady can be without having been one. So, it is interesting to read the comments of Jeannie Lo, who worked as an OL for Brother. Aside from the futility and frivolity of this particular lifestyle, it is evident that the economic contribution is quite meager:

> Mornings were slow times at the office. Sometimes the bosses gave women difficult assignments, but most of the time their work only took up two or three hours of the day. The bosses had managed Brother for decades and had not changed their views of worker roles. Men did the challenging work; OLs served tea, did light clerical work, and, as "office flowers," brightened up the office with their presence . . . they rarely mentioned their work. Few found their assigned clerical tasks to be thought-provoking or worthy of mention.[19]

This is a terrible waste of anyone's time in the office. The waste is often yet greater in the service sector, where a disproportionate number of women are employed. They frequently become salesgirls, serving ladies, hostesses, or other personnel who add little to the economy. Or they run the farms while the men are away. Hard work but not very useful given Japan's mediocre agricultural productivity.

Women workers are clearly being wasted. Does it matter? It probably matters very much because women are an increasingly large portion of the workforce. Over the years, the female participation rate has risen steadily to the point where, at present, about half of all women work, most of them in salaried jobs. Moreover, 37 percent of the total labor force consists of women.[20] It is certainly important to make better use of over one-third of the nation's workers and any country which fails to do this can hardly claim to be tops in management.

Will this change? Given the failure of the equal opportunity law, one may have legitimate doubts. So far, the men who run the companies show little interest in improving the situation, perhaps because they benefit from this discrimination. Also, many are too old to realize that times have changed and women expect better treatment. The only hope for progress is probably that, with growing tightness in the labor market, companies will be forced to hire more women and may eventually decide to use them more wisely. Then again, they may not. ■

Notes

1. See Kazukiyo Kurosawa, *Productivity Measurement of White Collar Workers*, Tokyo Institute of Technology, 1980.

2. See Whitehall and Takezawa, *The Other Worker*, pp. 196-205.

3. For interesting reflections on the role of Japanese managers, see Shunzo Arai, *An Intersection of East and West, Japanese Business Management*.

4. See Clark, *The Japanese Company*, and Rohlen, *For Harmony and Strength*.

5. For a broad perspective of decision-making in various sectors, see Vogel ed., *Modern Japanese Organization and Decision-Making*.

6. "Japanese Business Powwows," *World Executive Digest*, May 1986, p. 58.

7. Despite the general impression of loyalty, recent studies indicate that the Japanese are not as committed to their companies as hitherto assumed. See James R. Lincoln and Arne L. Kalleberg, *Culture, Control and Commitment*.

8. Harmony and loyalty have cultural roots, but they are not as deep or pervasive as commonly thought. Indeed, harmony was partially "invented" as a tool by prewar business leaders. See Kinzley, *Industrial Harmony in Modern Japan*.

9. *PHP*, December 1975, pp. 60-61.

10. See Lo, *Office Ladies, Factory Women*, and Kondo, *Crafting Selves*.

11. For more on social rapport in the factories, see Cole, *Japanese Blue Collar*, Dore, *British Factory—Japanese Factory*, and Kamata, *Japan in the Passing Lane*.

12. Ministry of Labor, *Handbook of Labor Statistics*, annual.

13. *Jitsugyo-no-Nihon*, December 1, 1978.

14. On their travails, see Akio Morita, *Made in Japan*, Eiji Toyoda, *Fifty Years in Motion*, and other books by more dynamic and entrepreneurial company founders and directors.

15. On the status of women workers in general, see Alice Cook and Hiroko Hayashi, *Working Women in Japan*, and Mary Saso, *Women in the Japanese Workplace*. On women in smaller companies or temporary employment, see Chalmers, *Industrial Relations in Japan*, and Kondo, *Crafting Selves*.

16. According to Saso, op. cit., this legislation failed to alter the situation of most women and equal opportunity remained a "sham," pp. 224-231.

17. Ministry of Labor, op. cit.

18. For a first-hand description of the careers of both blue-collar and white-collar female workers, see Lo, *Office Ladies, Factory Women*.

19. Ibid., pp. 42 and 48.
20. Ministry of Labor, *White Paper on Women*, annual.

4

The Management System Crumbles

Second Thoughts on Lifetime Employment

■ By now it seems that every foreigner must know about the "typical" Japanese management system. It is presented far and wide as the secret of Japan's economic success. You have lifetime employment (*shushinkoyo*), promotion by seniority (*nenko joretsu*), and annual pay increments. Since employees enjoy relatively similar treatment, they all progress gradually on the career escalator. With personnel remaining with the company throughout their whole career, it is willing to provide in-house training and takes in generalists rather than specialists. The cornerstone of the whole structure is loyalty to the company, whereby not only the management but the enterprise union show unusual dedication and abnegation, accept to work hard, promote the company's reputation, and see to it that it succeeds.

This system was supposedly in the best interest of all concerned, workers and management. This view, in a mildly edulcorated form, was presented by Ezra Vogel.

> The company's interest in the long term is also related to the system of permanent employment whereby an ordinary employee remains in the firm from the time he first enters after leaving school until he retires. . . . The firm is committed to the employee and provides a sense of belonging, personal support, welfare and retirement benefits, an increased salary and rank with age. Barring serious long-term depression, the employee expects that he will never be laid off, and even if the company were to disband or be absorbed by another company, he expects that a new job elsewhere will be arranged.[1]

The Japanese know that this idyllic picture is somewhat overdone, that the typical system only applies to the bigger companies and even there only includes regular workers. They know that there are imperfections and drawbacks. What worries them far more now is that the system itself is undergoing tremendous pressure and both management and labor are having second thoughts about the supposed advantages.

That there should be changes in this "typical" system is hardly surprising. After all, despite any insistence on its traditional roots, the system only came into existence after World War II. It had precedents before. But the present arrangements did not exist in Tokugawa Japan, in Meiji Japan, nor in prewar Japan. In fact, the system as such still does not exist in smaller companies or for the masses of temporary workers. Being less pervasive and systematic than claimed, it is natural that it could be shaken.

One decisive weakness has proven to be the Japanese management system's dependence on continuing rapid growth and economic boom. Since such conditions existed from shortly after the war until the first oil crisis, many seemed to think that they would last forever and thus the system could be maintained forever. However, no sooner did the drop in sales, the need to reduce staff, and uncertainty about future business trends appear than management itself began to question the merits of lifetime employment.

Obviously, when the economy was expanding, it was essential to bring in as many employees as possible and hold on to them for as long as possible. One could not afford to let them leave and have to train new ones. The switch into new products and sectors also made it useful to have generalists, who could be trained to do many things, and would not have a vested interest in a given job. With a young work force, it was financially advantageous to pay seniority-based wages because most of the employees were on the lower steps of the escalator. And, steady expansion meant that an employee's devotion could be more readily rewarded by promotion and wage hikes.

Now Japan's managers are discovering the disadvantages of the system. One that was bound to come anyway arose from the rapid aging of the population. All of a sudden, rather than most employees being on low wages, more were earning high ones so the companies were pricing themselves out of the market. With slower growth, they often quite simply had too much staff and had to oust some . . . loyalty or no loyalty. Here they encountered the resistance of the unions. From often bitter opponents of lifetime employment, which implied regimentation of labor, they switched to become its strongest supporters in the guise of "job security." But they were not enough to block the changes.

What then will happen to loyalty? Those who assume that loyalty is an inherent Japanese virtue may assume that it will not weaken. Those who know Japanese history better will realize that it is quite perishable and that the enormous fuss made about loyalty stems not from its spontaneous presence but the need to nurture it. As one of Japan's leading industrial sociologists, Kunio Odaka, explained:

> Only the uninformed outsider, or nationalist seeking something to extol in the Japanese character, could believe that all Japanese have some kind of innate loyalty that would prevent the disintegration of the company even if nothing were done to strengthen and consolidate personal relations.... Loyalty to the company is by no means an innate or instinctive Japanese trait. Today as in the past, Japanese who work for a company work for their own needs and interests. If they work willingly, it is because the work satisfies their own needs and does not involve any undue suffering or sacrifice. If forced to perform dull, repetitive, compartmentalized tasks in a mechanized or automated plant without any discretionary freedom, even the most diligent Japanese worker will eventually lose the will to work and fail to identify with the company.[2]

That is why the management system was carefully designed to enhance—if not impose—loyalty. Lifetime employment, in very subtle ways, creates a solid material foundation for that spiritual trait. It is encouraged palpably by higher wages for longer service. It is furthered by promotion from within the organization. And it is nourished by company entertainment, human relations, and welfare.

In addition, the whole company structure, loyalty and all, is built on people. It would come under serious pressure if the people changed. That is why company executives are closely following social and economic trends, many of which they find distinctly unnerving.

From Master Sergeant to Baby-Sitter

Japan's personnel officers have been through a lot in past years. Just after the war, when they had to enroll the masses of returning soldiers to rebuild the economy, they probably felt like master sergeants. Gradually, as the first peacetime generations arose, they adopted a position closer to that of a big brother. Then, with even younger classes, they switched to a pose not unlike that of a surrogate father. And now, when today's youngsters come of age, they may have to engage in a form of baby-sitting.

The change in the behavior of workers has been drastic and, as far as personnel officers are concerned, hardly encouraging. From year-to-year they welcome new batches of high school and university graduates and from year-to-year they find it harder to teach them the ropes and make them diligent and loyal workers, a situation which may be their own fault. Companies have always sought relatively pliable recruits who could be shaped to their own specific needs. Employers essentially wanted a blank piece of paper, not putty!

It was not very hard to direct the remnants of the prewar generations. They had been raised on patriotism and sacrifice. It was enough to show them the task, teach them the techniques, and then convince them of the importance of performing well. Those born during the war were less tough. After all, they had grown up in a time of thought control and, although they could follow instructions nicely, they sometimes lacked initiative. Even among those born shortly after the war, it was possible to find the essential human material to create good company men. The *moretsu shain* (dynamic employees imbued with a *samurai*-like spirit) did their best and are still at the forefront of every production and sales campaign.

But these company "warriors" are rapidly being replaced by very different types. First came the "my-home" and "new family" generations. These people were less interested in the job than the earnings it brought. They were working more for money than for patriotism or satisfaction. But burdened down with the cost of a house and maintaining the "new family" lifestyle, they could not slacken the pace much. At first they were in a minority compared with the *moretsu* types and would have looked bad if they too obviously showed reluctance to work hard.[3]

However, as far back as 1964, the majority of managers surveyed thought that young employees tended to work no more than was directly asked of them and that they lacked eagerness and interest in work. And more such employees joined the workforce all the time. By 1980, a Japan Recruit Center survey of male freshman employees showed that those who insisted that their main purpose in working was "to create a fulfilling and enjoyable home and family" outnumbered those who said "it is all right to sacrifice family life to some extent in order to put one's soul into the job" by more than two to one.[4] Thus, the workaholics were clearly being replaced by the "my-home" and "new family" generation.

The decline in interest in work continued. The postwar baby boomers were even less promising material. They had been pampered as children, given pretty much what they wanted with little effort to attain it, then overprotected in most inessentials while dominated in such important matters as education and marriage. They had little backbone and were often referred to as the *shirake sedai* (reactionless generation). After them came the *shinjinrui* or "new human race" in contrast to all that went before. They were even less interested in work and more in pleasure, less in others and more in themselves, than their predecessors.

Thus, the classes of selfless workaholics were replaced by classes of increasingly limp workers who no longer fit the traditional mold. First, as indicated, their attitudes toward work differed radically. They would do what the boss ordered, but little more, and even that without much good will. A job was no longer the most important thing in life; it had to make way for family life and personal pleasures. Younger workers wanted more free time and less after-hours work socializing.

The differences extended even further. Earlier generations had been very nationalistic and eager to contribute to society—a trait rapidly disappearing judging by the results of the periodic surveys of Japanese national character by the Institute of Statistical Mathematics. More and more people were interested in leading a carefree existence instead of contributing to society or leading a clean and honest life.[5]

Finally, despite greater individualism and even egoism, the traditional dependence syndrome, or *amae*, kept growing.[6] This was shown by another periodic survey, that of the Ministry of Education, which asked young people what sort of boss (*kacho*) they would like to serve under. The choice is between one who is relatively lenient at work but is otherwise unconcerned about the life of his subordinates and another who is demanding but "looks after people well outside of work." The latter had always been more popular. But during the 1980s, this preference attracted an overwhelming share of responses.[7]

It is hardly surprising that this kind of boss should appeal to a generation of youngsters that has grown used to living under protectors, whether mothers, teachers, or older colleagues. It is natural that they should look for someone to care for them at work as well. However, the problems that can arise from such an attitude are perfectly clear to some. According to a *Japan Times'* editorial: "Our interpretation of this desire is weakness. If so many workers want only to be taken care of—their bosses substituting for their nursing mothers, it seems—where are the leadership and initiative going to come from?"[8]

Alas, it is not only a question of leadership but also of suitable followers. For the *amae* urge does not always go coupled, as it did in the past, with a wish to reciprocate. Many youngsters feel that they have a "right" to be looked after without a corresponding "duty" to help others. This means that they could not be drawn into the traditional Japanese system. Decision-making from the bottom up or work in small groups with relative independence, which are the underpinnings of the system, would have trouble functioning even as well as they do now. It may no longer be possible to count on the voluntary efforts of ordinary workers and employees without making correspondingly greater efforts to gain their understanding and fire what little ambition remains.

On the other hand, there are some trends that show a positive interest in work. In listing reasons for choosing a job, more and more young people concentrate on the job itself rather than the company name or prestige. They prefer it because it is something they like to do, it takes advantage of the skills they have acquired, it is a challenge. Work, although frequently seen as a drab duty, is also regarded as a way of joining in society or leading a meaningful life by some. Surprisingly enough, many young people claim that they would gladly work diligently "because it will contribute to my self-attainment even if it fails to attract attention."

Normally, this attitude could work out very positively for companies as well if they knew how to harness the growing taste for initiative and challenge. But it is being turned into another negative by company executives. The Japanese management system, as presently constituted, simply is not geared to employees who want to seek their own paths rather than sticking to the career escalator and bowing to the rules of job rotation and seniority promotion. Thus, they have made enemies of potential allies in the vital task of adapting the system to today's new classes of workers. This was highlighted by one of Japan's leading management specialists, Keitaro Hasegawa.

A new breed of younger employees is leading the attack on the two institutions. In their view, the standardized track of regular promotions is overly egalitarian. Even though it offers them a firm guarantee of steadily increasing wages, which are now high by international standards, they feel that it does not give them adequate monetary recognition for their abilities as individuals. They have even begun to see promotion by seniority as an intolerable constraint. And because the current brisk economic expansion has made job opportunities plentiful, they are quitting their companies for employment elsewhere, elevating the rate of labor mobility.[9]

Jumping Off the Escalator

Young people no longer seem quite so eager to stay on the career escalator nowadays. Of course, they want a good job. Of course, they want to get into good companies. This means almost by definition that they will be a tiny cog in a huge machine and that they will be put on an escalator that looks more like a conveyor belt. But what is new is that many of them, after a short ride, think very seriously of getting off. And more of them eventually do.

When they first visit the company, they repeat pat phrases like "I am here because I think I can serve your company," or "I have come because I think highly of your company." But everyone knows that they make such statements because they want the job. Before they came, however, the candidates looked very carefully into the situation of the company, its wage scale, the chances of promotion, its relations with other companies, its hopes of survival. Actually, wanting to serve the company was considerably less important than finding out if it would be able to look after them properly during a long career.

This is shown most by the meticulous way in which they rank companies and the feeling that, although fresh out of school, with no experience and few skills, there are a vast number of companies that rank so low they would not set foot there. Even among those they deign to visit, there is a clear priority. Their good will decreases as the ranking falls, although they may accept the job.

By the way, the trends of company ranking have been very clear over the past decade. Ever fewer students want to enter manufacturing and more and more opt for services like banking, securities, advertising, or leisure. They definitely prefer comfortable office jobs to those in factories or warehouses. At the bottom of the list are the "three-K" jobs, those which are *kitanai*, *kiken*, and *kitsui* or dirty, dangerous, and demanding. Just about everybody wants to get into a big company; just about nobody wants to join a small company.

This is mentioned because, despite their best efforts, most new recruits end up in companies that are not at the top of their list. This is quite natural. Since everyone chooses the same leading companies, only a small minority can possibly get in while the rest go to their second, third, or last choice.

With most going to companies which are *not* their first, or even second choice, it is not surprising that many eventually become discontent. In interviews and polls, they express dissatisfaction with their bosses, their colleagues, their specific tasks, their hours, their salaries, and so on. Naturally, they usually keep this to themselves since they may have to stick with their employer anyway. But the discipline and abnegation of earlier generations is rapidly disappearing. Today's employees increasingly decide that the best solution is to change jobs.

Changing jobs (*tenshoku*) is still a serious matter. Companies do not like to lose personnel, even young personnel, whom they have trained and entrusted with responsibility. And other companies as a rule tend to prefer hiring their own fresh recruits rather than picking up mid-career personnel, especially those with a record of job-hopping. Nonetheless, it is not terribly difficult to find a job, especially for young people, when there is a relative labor shortage. As Iwao Shimizu, president of Coordinate Center, an employment agency, explained:

> Young people are particularly sensitive to changing social currents, and are aware of the increasingly business-like relationships which have evolved between companies and their employees. If one's company or immediate superiors do not appreciate one's talents, the solution is to find a new employer who will. Younger people feel that this approach is quicker and more effective than the traditional one of waiting.[10]

However, while changing jobs is becoming more widespread among younger workers, it is still less noticeable among older employees. In part, the reason is the greater sense of discipline or indoctrination that exists amongst the older population. It is also based on cold calculation. Changing jobs can be very costly since, having ridden the career escalator part way up, an employee would normally have to start further down or even at the bottom with a new employer. This would entail a loss of status and, even more telling, earnings. How much can be lost was computed by Asahi Mutual Life Insurance. Changing jobs at the age of 25 would cost a worker about 14 percent of his lifetime income.[11] Changing jobs at 35 would involve a loss of some 28 percent. This is undoubtedly a strong deterrent.

Thus, while job-hopping is still much smaller than in the West, it is steadily growing according to official statistics. Indeed, in 1990, some 4.2 percent of the workforce changed jobs and employers griped about a "*tenshoku* boom."[12] That the trend is likely to continue was indicated by an interesting survey by the Japan Chamber of Commerce which showed that many Japanese students had little desire to stay with a company for life. As many as 31 percent said they might change their job some time and fully 19 percent thought of running their own business.[13]

What is equally preoccupying is that, despite the huge number of job offers, so many young people are remaining unemployed. The unemployment rate for high school graduates is three times the national level and, for university graduates, twice as high. This has given rise to what is called the "non-worker syndrome." The top reason both for changing jobs or refusing jobs is overwhelmingly "the work does not suit me," according to a Ministry of Labor survey.[14]

While less noticeable than job-hopping and non-working, there is a rapidly growing category of what the Japanese dubbed *furita* or "freeter." This word is concocted from the English word "free" and the German word *"Arbeiter"* or worker and implies temporary employee. Most "freeters" got into temporary work during their school days and decided that they preferred it instead of a full-time lifelong occupation. They can usually earn about as much as regular employees but don't have to bother with company rules, discipline, and pressure and can quit any time they want and then look for another job.[15]

There is much talk, perhaps more abroad than in Japan, that this is a passing phase or that once employees have been acclimated, they will be as eager and active as past generations. This is far from certain since the two primary advantages of lifetime employment are shrinking. Given the difficulty in obtaining young workers, salaries have risen much more rapidly for that category than for older workers. So the earnings differential based on seniority is diminishing. Worse, it is increasingly possible to sell one's skills on the labor market. This is particularly true for specialists who are snapped up by companies entering new sectors.

The other benefit that held employees was the promise of promotion. Once it was almost axiomatic that if you stayed on the career escalator long enough you would rise to a position of responsibility. While this was never absolute and not everyone got a title, the fact that one had a relatively good chance of becoming a section head (*kacho*) or department head (*bucho*) was enough. Also, even if you did get a title, it was not certain that you actually had enhanced authority, let alone a larger pay package. Over the years, however, with fewer employees entering at the bottom, there was less need for bosses at the top. According to the Economic Planning Agency, in a survey entitled "Japan's Labor Market in the Year 2000," only one out of every four male college graduates would make it to *kacho* or *bucho* at the end of the century.[16] Those odds were no longer good enough to tie one to the company.

Worse, among youngsters born in the postwar baby boom, interest in being promoted lessened significantly. This was revealed by a survey of the Management and Coordination Agency. Some 29 percent of the respondents stated they were not enthusiastic about being promoted and another 31 percent said they did not care much about promotion as long as they could demonstrate their abilities at work. Of the rest, 6 percent felt they would not be promoted even if they tried and, of those who sought promotion, 17 percent hoped to achieve this by working no harder than average while just 6 percent were willing to make greater efforts[17]—hardly a generation of eager beavers!

Obviously, more frequent job changes is not just a fad among more recent classes of employees. There have been fundamental modifications in workers' attitudes which encourage them to question lifetime employment. Meanwhile, the possibilities of alternate employment have grown and so has public acceptance of job-hopping. If Japan's employers do not respond appropriately, the *tenshoku* boom could get out of hand.

Pushed Off the Escalator

There is a bitter irony about Japan's present employment situation. No country in the world makes so much fuss about loyalty to the company and seniority. Nowhere else is there as much lip service about not firing personnel in general and caring for older ones in particular. Yet, whenever the economy slows down, who are the first to be discarded? . . . the older employees!

It is thus not surprising to find particularly serious problems at the upper end of the escalator. Unlike the problems of younger employees, older employees do not seem to concern the company so much, at least not at first glance. After all, the company is trying to ease them out, not keep them in. So, after some token support and a few words of encouragement, much of the burden rests on the shoulders of the older men themselves. And those who bore the brunt of this were not the ordinary workers, the rank-and-file, since they were largely backed by the unions. It was the older salarymen, those who did not make it to titular posts (and some who did) and expected the better times promised them when they were young.

The first problem is the official retirement age. It was originally set at 55, back in 1902, when the average life expectancy was only 42. Now it has increased to well over 75. Thus, 55 is a bit young. This was recognized by larger companies especially, which raised the age to 57 or even 60. But the amount of retirement benefits was not raised sufficiently to cover the many, long years. Worse, public pension schemes only begin at 60 and the government has threatened to hike the age to 65.

How then should retirees get by? Company pensions often consisted of a lump sum severance payment equal to a few years' wages. Others have annuities now, but they are equally modest. Public pension schemes are not much better and there is very little public welfare. Thus, the alternative is between a very stringent retirement and working longer to round out any income. No wonder a post-retirement job is increasingly a must. It is not only a matter of keeping busy, but of survival. That explains why Japan still has many more workers above the age of 60 than in the West.[18]

If at least one could count on working until 55 or 60, there would be worries but not acute anxiety. Alas, despite the supposed prevalence of lifetime employment, companies are finding all sorts of ways of getting rid of employees earlier. Since there is some residual protection of regular staff, many of the techniques are quite ingenious . . . and devious.

There is the "golden handshake" which allows a man to step down with pride . . . but still no job. When times get worse, there is the "tap-on-the-shoulder" and the offer of a modest bonus to withdraw gracefully. This, too, accomplishes the task rather well. For the salarymen know that the next time they get a "tap-on-the-shoulder" the bonus will be much smaller and it is even possible that they will simply be fired. If not, they may wind up transferred to an unpleasant provincial or overseas office, or put in a low-level subsidiary, or sent to the sales division, or demoted to an awkward position with colleagues and even superiors who are younger than they. These steps are usually combined with a freeze or reduction in wages.

Strangely enough, those in the most precarious position are the middle managers. Although theoretically enjoying a higher status than ordinary workers, they are not defended by the unions and are thus more exposed to pressure from top management. It is in the ranks of middle managers that the real "weight reduction" has been taking place. Many of the plans have included the alternative of early retirement with increasingly large bonuses the younger one voluntarily retires. But this is just a generalization of the "selective retirement" that has been around ever since the oil crisis. Those between the ages of 40 and 50 who are willing to step down are offered incentives as a carrot. The stick is that their wages rise more slowly or not at all. Truly recalcitrant ones may be demoted or given a "specialist" post to get them out of the way.

There is probably no doubt in the minds of the older men that a method will be found. Thus, many of them become quite nervous and despondent. Yet, even then, they accept the humility of being relegated to what the Japanese call the "window-sill tribe" or *madogiwa zoku*. These are employees with a desk near the window and no real work, who stare out the window while awaiting their fate. On the other hand, some salarymen make a desperate effort to regain status by proving their value and ability to the company. If that does not work, they begin brushing up on their accounting techniques, or learning a simple trade, or studying the job market just in case they can land a job elsewhere.

Alas, when they do find themselves back in the job market, at the age of 40 and over, with nothing else to recommend them than that they worked for a pretty big company for over 20 years, the older ex-employees will be in a harder position than the youngsters fresh out of school. Whereas most school leavers can expect the equivalent of three job openings each, the opposite holds for older people who find themselves two or three to one opening. Whereas the younger candidates can hope to enter reasonably good companies, these older losers are excluded and must accept the smallest companies and often the lowliest of tasks.

This is often a tragedy. It is not easy to start a new job at that age, especially in a society that looks down on those who have lost their job and has trouble absorbing newcomers. It is painful to pass from a big to a smaller company. And it is far harder to endure an often lowly position after having enjoyed the prestige of relatively senior posts, or at least accumulated seniority, elsewhere. Young salarymen may joke about the middle managers who have become clerks, salesmen, or even janitors. For those concerned, it is anything but a joking matter.

The basic reason that companies are now trying to squeeze out the older employees is that, with seniority pay, they are earning considerably more than younger people although they lack the vitality, do not always have the same level of education, and their contribution is deemed inadequate to justify the pay. It was, of course, the company that offered supplements for staying with it, and thus the company that is responsible for the wage differentials and which should, in theory, accept to honor these debts now that they fall due. Perhaps the company would like to; perhaps it doesn't really care. In any event, companies have a perfect excuse to renege on old promises whenever business is slow.

Whatever the excuse, this is also a direct attack on lifetime employment. First of all, it makes a mockery of the nation's creed and traditions that unemployment should be most serious among older people. It is particularly ugly because the social security and welfare system was never built up enough to meet the present needs. Thus, older, unemployed people may find themselves in a financial pinch unless aided by friends and relatives. But the depths of Japan's shame is that those who are suffering most are the very ones who were responsible for raising the economy from the rubble and creating the affluence that now prevails. Many of these people are patriots of a sort. But their reward is to be asked one last service, namely to sacrifice themselves for the sake of the company and a society that will not care adequately for them.

This cavalier treatment of older employees also affects the rest of the staff. By discarding those for whom the seniority arrangements were created, the companies are admitting to both older *and* younger workers that their word cannot be trusted. Whereas once they could call for loyalty and this would seem only fair, by showing their disloyalty to those who had served them longest they will hardly be able to inculcate loyalty in a younger generation for whom such appeals are suspicious anyway. Given the importance of social and human relations in Japanese companies, even the slightest hint that one may be demoted or discarded some time is enough to break the emotional ties and result in worsening performance.

Meanwhile, the treatment of older employees is having an unexpected impact on middle-aged ones. They are beginning to consider their options much earlier. The more capable and dynamic ones are among the first to accept any offer of early retirement. And some are quitting anyway when they find an interesting alternative. Less capable, less dynamic employees are busy currying favor and appearing to keep occupied so that they will not be asked to leave. The result is that the quality of the company's human resources is gradually declining and it may be stuck with lots of dead wood.

Kacho-byo and Other Illnesses

According to most Japanese, the truly decisive level in the hierarchy is middle management. Unlike the Western-style pyramid, where top management tries to maintain full control over the workings of the company, much of the power is delegated to the *bucho* (department head), and by him to the various *kacho* (section heads), and on down. Not only is the power delegated, in many cases middle managers are quite simply left to figure out how things should be done and held responsible for the results. Top management looks on, makes comments, but does not really intervene unless there are noticeable difficulties.

The middle managers thus provide the essential level at which overall policy is sorted out into day-to-day activities and where decisions are actually implemented. Although basic goals and policies come from above, as well as many specific orders, the middle managers also have to liaise among themselves to provide a suitable framework for overall action. Below them, power is also delegated, and sometimes just diffused, but there is no one who gathers as many vital strings together.

This makes the middle management, and especially the *kacho*, the decisive link in the company structure. They are where everything comes together. And they have a multitude of responsibilities, both administrative and social.

Their normal administrative work is quite considerable and not very different from a Western "boss." They have to decide which individual or group in their section will be entrusted with which task. With the loose job classification that exists, this may also imply helping to decide how the work should be done even in its practical details. They must check on the implementation and results, for they will ultimately reap the praise for successful accomplishment or bear the blame for mistakes. They have to see to it that cooperation, as opposed to overlapping, duplication, or competition, arises with other sections.

But, in addition to directing and guiding, the *kacho* also have their own work to do. They have to deal with customers, bargain with suppliers, or make arrangements for work that is contracted out. In the sales division, for example, the *kacho* not only has to keep an eye on the other salesmen, he has to handle his own clients, usually the biggest and most important.

This is not all. The *kacho* also plays a vital social role. In order to get the most out of his subordinates, he has to show a kindly interest in their work and even their personal life. He may have to help them out of some difficulty, in the company or outside. This is then capped with a friendly drink after work or a periodic dinner with his younger colleagues so that they can get to know one another better than office protocol permits. However, as a salaryman he also ends up drinking with the clients and suppliers. And, as an inferior, very concerned about keeping up good relations with top management, he would not turn down an invitation to dine with the *bucho* or others higher up.

Socializing is a very time-consuming occupation. It is not always a pleasant one, depending on who one sees and how often it must be done. By now many *kacho* regard this as a duty more than a pleasure and a "necessary evil" in the view of some. But it is made more painful by the fact that today's *kacho* are among the last Japanese who have much understanding of what Japan used to be like and can suitably deal with their superiors who are rapidly becoming fossils of another era. They are certainly not on the same wave length as their subordinates but at least they recognize the tune.

So, the *kacho* have to establish communications between those on top and those further down. As hinted, this is not very easy. They pass along the watchwords of loyalty, dedication, company spirit and the like, but they know the younger employees often snicker. They then try to explain to the stodgy old men why young people no longer want to put in overtime or sacrifice home life. It is an ungrateful task and brings them little benefit.

All this makes the *kacho* and some other middle managers the hardest working and most harassed personnel. They put in long days at work with no extra pay for overtime. They then put in long evenings at entertainment, sometimes at their own expense. They not only have to be competent in their own job but also reasonably popular with their colleagues and subordinates. They have almost no personal hobbies and no real home life. And they do not even take more than a few days vacation. This makes them the last of the workaholics.

But at least the *kacho* had his title and his job. He also had legitimate hopes of promotion. That is, until the 1980s. For it was suddenly realized that there was too much dead wood in managerial circles. Over the years, the career escalator has been forwarding many middle-aged people onto the level at which one is usually appointed manager. Obviously, no matter how rapidly the company expanded, there was not enough room for them all. So the company began inventing new and often pointless posts, even if they involved no special tasks or responsibilities nor even a rise in pay, but merely gave the man a title. This army of managers, from assistant chiefs on up, tended to get in one another's way and it was necessary to clarify the lines of command. The easiest way of doing so was simply to get rid of some of them.

The rationalization then went a bit further. Obviously, not all the *kacho* could make it to *bucho*, and not all the *bucho* could become directors, nor all the directors, presidents. Rather than have them swelling the ranks of superfluous staff or kept on the payroll with little to do, a screening was introduced at managerial levels. Those who could progress further would be left on the escalator, the others shoved off. They would then be given the alternative of staying on in the company, often as a specialist or professional with a lower status and salary, or retiring and trying to make good elsewhere. Fitness to become a manager would be determined by informal methods and occasionally a promotion examination. A few companies even experimented with a "term" system whereby managers would be appointed for a fixed tenure and dismissed if they proved inadequate.

So, added to all his other headaches, the middle manager had serious worries as to whether he would succeed. Sometimes he felt he was being watched too carefully by those who would decide his fate. At other times he was really in the hot seat, as the head of a profit center, and if he could not make profits well enough he might be on the way out. This generated what was commonly called the *kacho-byo* (*kacho*'s disease). Although a psychological and moral ailment, it also had physical ramifications. Increasing numbers of managers complained of ulcers and heart trouble.

Recently a more virulent strain of the same illness has emerged, afflicting many middle managers but also younger employees. It resulted in what is widely known as *karoshi* or death from overwork. It is impossible to ascertain how many workers have been struck down. One authority, Hiroshi Kawahito, a lawyer specializing in *karoshi* cases, estimated as many as 10,000 a year.[19] But it could be more, much more, since the companies and

Ministry of Labor colluded to keep such cases from being declared in order to avoid paying compensation.

Whatever the number, three things are certain. One is that *karoshi* results from excessive overwork and nervous stress deriving from company life. Another is that countless Japanese feel the symptoms to some degree. A survey by Fukoku Life Insurance showed that about 70 percent of the respondents felt "stressed," 44 percent suffered from constant fatigue, 28 percent lacked creativity and motivation and 23 percent wanted to call in sick. The third conclusion is that the fear of death by overwork is widespread and rapidly growing as was stated by 43 percent of the workers surveyed.[20]

These problems could not help affecting the company. By making the middle managers the scapegoats for difficulties and putting them under pressure, the crucial link in the hierarchy was being made a weak link. Middle managers could simply not perform as they were supposed to under these conditions.

No Reply from the Top

No matter how important competent workers in the factories and offices may be, or how essential it is to have capable middle managers, it is obvious that one also needs intelligent leadership from the top. Top management must decide on basic and long-term policy that will be implemented by all other levels. And, if it decides unwisely, it is not only the efforts of all the rest of the staff that will be wasted. Since they are schooled in harmony and loyalty, and will implement foolish policy as vigorously as wise policy, the whole company could be endangered.

Descriptions of the Japanese management system usually dwell at length on the activities at lower levels. How the workers are motivated and create QC circles. How the salarymen engage in decision-making and write *ringisho*. How the *kacho* brings out the best in his men and strives for the company's success. But pitifully little is ever said about top management, aside from praising the glorious leadership of such-and-such a president. Very little is known about how he actually directs the company or who in the company actually controls the levers of command.[18] Worse, almost nothing is known about the problems encountered at the top or those directors whose leadership has been merely competent, less than acceptable, or outright disastrous.

Nevertheless, it should be clear from the basic characteristics of the management system that it is extremely hard to control things from above. The fact that the basic unit is the group, as opposed to the individual, simplifies things somewhat since one has to work with fewer elements. However, the group is a very tight organism, concerned with its own success and prerogatives, and thus has to be handled gently. Many of them are relatively independent until they can be convinced to fall into line with overall policy. Should this policy not favor them, then the *nemawashi* can take endlessly long. Moreover, efforts at bringing all groups into line alternate with periods when they are purposely encouraged to compete against one another. Their leaders are also potential rivals in the race for promotions. All this is compounded by the fact that in Japanese companies, groups can be very small and amazingly numerous.

Those particular factors make it hard to impose strong control downward or even routine coordination except in rather special cases or when the entire company can be whipped into a crisis mentality or aligned against its competitors. They also make the whole decision-making process more complicated than necessary. Many top managers do not take hard-and-fast decisions on their own and then simply impose them. At best they engage in careful *nemawashi*. But in far more cases, the decision-making process is very dispersed, among the various top managers, the middle managers, and sometimes with an input from below. At the same time, top management not only handles broad company policy but frequently has to deal with quite minor matters that have filtered up from below and need approval. Whereas the diffuse type of decision-making so popular in Japan shows its advantages at lower and middle levels, it is just as likely to reveal its drawbacks at the top.

One reason the weaknesses of top management have not been very noticeable so far is that many decisions during the earlier period of reconstruction and growth were relatively simple and straightforward. It was necessary to enter a given field, make a given product, and sell it actively. The whole staff, from top to bottom, could be geared to this. And the basic slogan was to fight and to fight hard. In an economy with fewer opportunities to be followed up aggressively, where caution is needed in making investments, and balance required to obtain profits, the slogans become more ambivalent—fight as hard as you can, but if necessary hold back and perhaps even retreat. These are not the sort of orders business leaders like to give, and they are apparently confusing to their subordinates who are unable to decide when to push and when to fall back. It results in a stop-and-go approach that is very unsteady and hard to maintain.

Perhaps the greatest strength of Japanese managers is to know their company thoroughly. Being rotated periodically, passing from one sector or division to another, they become acquainted with a broad range of activities. They will also get to know many of their colleagues. This creates managers with exceptional ability at using the company machinery as well as obtaining support from their own network of personal relations. This in many ways makes up for any lacks in the decision-making process, because close cooperation is much easier among a group of managers who have worked their way slowly up the spiral staircase together.

But it does not obviate all the problems. One is that, although managers know much of the organization, they are still most closely related to one part or another. The *bucho* are obviously best acquainted with their own staff and problems and just as obviously try to defend their department's interest also against those of others. This they continue to do as directors, even though by then they should rather be thinking of the best interests of the company as a whole. Even when they become managing directors or presidents, many executives have been so impregnated with the concerns of the departments they know best and the personnel they have dealt with most that their policy can be biased. They are too busy paying off old debts to think what this may mean to company policy.

In addition, since they have risen to the top through the ranks, few of them know anything about *management* as such. They are often excellent sales people, or excellent production people, or excellent research people, but absolutely horrible managers when they reach a level where running the company as a whole is their primary task. It is common knowledge that the higher a person rises, the harder it is to decide whether he can take the next step. Many ordinary salarymen can become quite competent *kacho* and the average *kacho* might turn out reasonably well as a *bucho*. But a company would be very foolish to assume that more than a minority of the *bucho* could go any further. As of that level, the type of work changes radically and the decisions become so crucial that a mistake can be disastrous.

Despite this, as for middle managers, the present system does not really allow top managers to concentrate on their basic tasks either. The men at the top must also engage actively in the work of morale building and human relations. The managing directors have to maintain very close relations with the middle managers, both to direct and to evaluate them. The president and chairman are often so busy with social and quasi-political activities that they hardly have time for business as such. They must act as arbitrator for any disputes within the company. They have to appear as a father figure at numerous company functions. They spend untold hours entertaining major customers, keeping up relations with dealers, and seeing that subcontractors tow the line. For major companies, especially with government contacts, they join in *zaikai* activities and try to win the favor of influential politicians or bureaucrats.

Here, too, is a job which is so demanding that few could possibly accomplish it well. Either the business side must suffer or human relations must be neglected. It often happens that the top managers shift the burden of day-to-day decisions to the managing directors while they worry about rapport. This policy is a wise one if the other managers are up to the task. But too many presidents and chairmen nowadays neglect, or lack time to handle, what elsewhere would be their primary concern. Rather than controlling or dominating their own company, they become a figurehead for those actively running things. In fact, it is almost as if they had retired and just hang on as a symbol of authority. This can be beneficial by giving those lower down more leeway and encouraging initiative. It can also be harmful if managers do not entirely agree and there is no one person who knows enough to impart unity to the company's policy or force everyone to pull together.

These are problems which affect most companies in Japan, large or small, new or old. They have been around for a long time, and one would assume that the Japanese have become accustomed to dealing with them. Unfortunately, they are entering a more acute phase for two reasons: age and ability.

One of the most noticeable characteristics of Japanese executives, a direct consequence of seniority promotion, is their sheer age. According to the *Japan Economic Journal*, the average age of new presidents appointed in 1991 was just over 58. With an average stint of about nine years, this means that the people running Japan's companies are in their early sixties. And many of them then become company chairmen while in their seventies.[21] That is a far cry from American and European CEOs, where sixty or seventy is the exception. Not only are these aged "leaders" more likely to be physically and mentally over the hill, they have little understanding of or liking for many of the present trends in Japanese society.

More important than age is ability. Here, Japan is at an even more crucial turning point. It has reached the stage where the giants of the business world who brought about the economic miracle are disappearing. Whatever some may think, the bureaucratic leader is not typical of Japan's managers. Just after the war, the *zaibatsu* and major companies were disintegrated and many old leaders forcibly retired. Younger men had to take over. And only dynamic managers could restore the company's strength. At the same time, some older companies began to grow, either under the founder or his children. And a number of vital companies were first created. Most of the leaders who have become famous since were in those groups.

However, those strong and dynamic leaders cultivated the present crop of bureaucratic leaders. These are men who followed the slow path upward, who obeyed instructions, who made proper contacts, but who rarely showed initiative, imagination, or drive. They are admirable followers, some of the finest in the world. Now the time has come for Japan to find out if they are also capable leaders. There is considerable fear that these men may not meet expectations to judge by the number of companies that cling to their founders or older presidents. There is just as much reason to fear that by the time they become leaders they are quite simply too old. ■

Notes

1.   Vogel, *Japan As Number One*, p. 137.

2.   Odaka, *Japanese Management-A Forward-Looking Analysis*, p. 26.

3. For more on generational changes, see Woronoff, *Japan: The (Coming) Economic Crisis.*

4. "What do freshmen employees think?," Japan Recruit Center, 1980.

5. See Sumiko Iwao, "Recent Changes in Japanese Attitudes," in Alan D. Romberg and Tadashi Yamamoto eds., *Same Bed, Different Dreams,* pp. 41-66.

6. This was elucidated by Takeo Doi, *The Anatomy of Dependence.*

7. Management and Coordination Agency, *White Paper on Youth.*

8. *Japan Times,* October 7, 1979.

9. Keitaro Hasegawa, "The Upheavel in Personnel Management," *Japan Echo,* Vol. XVII, 1990, p. 23.

10. *Tokyo Business Today,* September 1988, p. 28.

11. *Japan Economic Journal,* August 30, 1986.

12. *Yomiuri,* July 27, 1991.

13. *Japan Economic Journal,* May 11, 1991.

14. See Mieko Watanabe, "Job Mobility and Work Attitudes of Young Workers," *Japan Labor Bulletin,* February 1, 1991, pp. 4-8.

15. See Yamane Kazuma, "Recruit and the Age of the Temporary Worker," *Japan Echo,* Vol. XVII, 1990, pp. 42-47.

16. *Japan Economic Journal,* June 25, 1985, p. 43.

17. *Mainichi,* September 19, 1989.

18. See Ministry of Labor, *Survey of Japanese Employees' Life After Retirement,* annual.

19. "Dropping in Harness," *Far Eastern Economic Review*, April 25, 1991.

20. "Japan's Overworked Workers," *Wall Street Journal*, November 29, 1990.

21. *Japan Economic Journal*, June 22, 1991.

5

Burdening Down the Economy

Shift from Primary to Tertiary

■ So far, we have encountered some of Japan's "wasted workers" in the offices of the very same companies whose factories are quite impressive. The largest contingents, however, can be found virtually everywhere outside the manufacturing sector. They are legion in farming, construction, and the service industry. This is obviously debilitating for Japan's economy, but it is particularly worrisome when one considers the fundamental changes taking place in that economy.

Ever since Japan began industrializing more than a century ago, manufacturing had been occupying an ever larger share of total production. However, that share peaked by the 1970s, with about 38 percent of the total. Since then it has been falling off and dropped to under 30 percent by the late 1980s. Similar trends can be observed for the production of goods, which includes agriculture, mining, manufacturing, and construction. The share slipped from about 53 percent in 1970 to about 43 percent at present. The slack was taken up by services (distribution, finance, insurance, real estate, transport, communications, and others). Their share rose from 47 percent in 1970 to 57 percent now.[1]

This shift naturally affected the employment structure. In fact, the changes in the composition of the workforce have been substantial. Over the same two decades, from 1970 to 1990, employment in the primary sector declined from 17 percent to 7 percent, dipped slightly in the secondary sector, from 35 percent to 34 percent, but compensated by expanding considerably in the tertiary sector, rising from 48 percent to 59 percent.[2] These trends merely prolonged earlier ones shown in Table 5.1.

Still, the shift in employment did not always coincide with the shift in production and this already reveals some pockets of "wasted" workers. For example, farmers only represent about 7 percent of the workforce. Alas, they generate less than 3 percent of gross domestic product, which makes their contribution rather paltry. Workers in the nation's factories more than justified their efforts. But those in the tertiary sector produced somewhat less GDP than would be expected of their large share in employment. They, too, were underachieving, if not quite as dramatically as the farmers.

What can be said about these significant shifts? Well, the first thing is obviously that they are not unusual and tend to occur in every country as it passes from the agricultural to the industrial

Table 5.1

Structure of Employment

	Composition (%)		
Year	Primary	Secondary	Tertiary
1950	48	22	30
1960	30	28	42
1970	17	35	48
1980	10	35	55
1990	7	34	59

Source: Bank of Japan

stage and gradually expands into services. Similar trends could be found in Western countries as well. But it should be noted that Japan's agricultural population is still on the high side and the share of those in manufacturing is sinking faster than in some other OECD nations. For the tertiary sector, all indications are that its share of employment will continue growing and gradually catch up with Europe, if not necessarily the United States.[3]

Is this good? According to many economists, it is. There is need for some sector to generate jobs for those who leave farming and industry, where increased production and efficiency require fewer workers. Moreover, the tertiary sector makes considerable contributions both to the productivity of other sectors and an enhanced quality of life for all. The wave of the future is a larger tertiary sector and there is no point in fighting it. To the contrary, it should be welcomed as a sign of maturity. After all, or so its proponents argue, the most advanced countries have service economies.

Still, it is uncertain whether this argument should be accepted in general or in particular, with regard to Japan. First of all, too much of the growth in Japan's tertiary sector appears to be related less to a need for workers than the ability of ever more people to slip into loosely organized, broadly dispersed, and labor-intensive areas. Secondly, as noted, the tertiary sector is not very productive, certainly not as compared to manufacturing from whence many of the employees come. Worse, productivity growth in some parts of distribution and services has been very disappointing. The broader question, though, is whether the move toward a service-based economy is a sign of maturity and progress or aging and decline.

That is why it is essential to take a much closer look at these various sectors and the "wasted workers" who inhabit them. In so doing, it does not hurt to mull over three general reflections. First, isn't it rather silly for Japan to work so hard at enhancing productivity of the smaller portion of workers while ignoring the larger? Secondly, if there are going to be ever more workers in the tertiary sector, won't this blunt the overall effort to strengthen and upgrade the economy? Finally, if present trends are not rectified, couldn't Japan be on the path to decline rather than progress?

Putting Farm Productivity Off for Tomorrow

In the case of Japanese agriculture, it hardly makes any sense to speak of productivity because the sector is plagued by both low productivity and high production levels.[4] This may seem strange at first, for Japan is incapable of growing enough agricultural produce to keep its population fed and its industries supplied with raw materials. It depends very heavily on imports to make up the difference, so much so that this is a heavy financial drain. But its most serious problem lies not where it cannot produce enough but where it produces too much.

Much of the present agricultural crisis arises from rice production, where the farmers have done too well. From year to year, the demand for rice has fallen as people have a more varied diet and especially as bread replaced the old "staple," rice. This, however, has not prevented the farmers from growing too much rice and showing great ingenuity in boosting yields per acre. Unfortunately, even using the finest methods and the best inputs, they cannot compete with the poor peasants of Southeast Asia or mechanized farmers in the West. So local production remains much more expensive than imports, with Japan's rice price six times that of the United States and nine times the level in Thailand.

This cost is actually too much for the Japanese population to bear and the government has had to take a position between the suppliers and purchasers. Unlike most middlemen, however, the state does not make a profit. It is obliged to sell the rice at a relatively low price so that it can be purchased by ordinary consumers. At the same time, it has been obliged to pay a rather high price to the farmers in order to cover the rising cost of inputs and keep farm income up to a "decent" level. This subsidy is not quite the end of it, since production has outstripped demand so much that rice stocks accumulate and have to be stored at great expense.

These subsidies, which mount from year to year, have proven to be a heavy burden on the government and, of course, on the average citizen and taxpayer. They are also a perfectly futile exercise since the government is in effect paying the farmers to produce rice no one wants. To cut back on this burden, measures have been taken to bring about a "production adjustment." In this way, the farmers would keep some of their land out of rice production in return for a different kind of subsidy. If they were willing to grow other crops instead, the government would help subsidize that venture. Since wheat was replacing rice in the people's diet, one prime target was to boost local production of wheat. However, since wheat is best grown in a highly mechanized and extensive manner, Japanese producers could not possibly compete with American or Canadian producers. To encourage them properly, a wheat subsidy was introduced that is rapidly growing in size and has added to the burden of the rice subsidy.

The situation for a number of other crops is just as bad, although it takes a slightly different form. Japan's fruit and vegetable growers are rarely as cheap or productive as their competitors abroad. This applies to many things, including cherries, oranges, and bananas. Thus, in order to keep the local price high enough to be remunerative, quotas and tariffs are raised to keep foreign produce out. At the same time, since local production is not enough to meet demand, imports are channeled through government purchasing agencies and private distributors in such a way that they are bought cheaply abroad and sold more expensively in Japan in order not to depress the market price. The most extreme case involves meat purchasing, which has already caused quite a scandal both domestically, due to the exorbitant prices charged, and abroad, since major trading partners sell their produce at the low going rate but can only export smaller quantities due to quotas or artificially high prices.

Some of the money collected by the government is channelled back to the producers in the form of assistance to raise productivity . . . if they want to. But the results have been rather modest. Although quantities produced have risen, the costs apparently have not fallen enough to end subsidies and protection. In a number of cases there is good reason to doubt whether Japan could ever be competitive. As long as the farms are small and there are limits to mechanization, it is impossible to achieve much. That is why, at present, productivity in agriculture is only one-quarter that of manufacturing when measured by current prices. But it must be remembered that Japan's bloated prices are about four times world levels. Thus, according to Kunitaro Takeda, an agricultural researcher, one-sixteenth would be a more valid comparison to manufacturing productivity.[5]

This situation could only be improved if each farmer were able to cultivate a larger area and could increase mechanization and efficiency. At present, the average farm is only a bit more than a hectare large, or about as big as a soccer field. Farms in Britain are about 50 times that size and in the United States, 150 times. But larger farms would only be possible if more farmers would sell or lease their land. That they have not done so is easy to understand. Farm land is taxed at exceptionally low rates and crops are subsidized, so why not farm . . . while waiting for the land's value to appreciate? That explains why only 12 percent of farmers live exclusively from farming while the rest only do it as a side job. This may change as farmers age and die, but progress has been slow.[6]

The other obstacle to modernizing agriculture is that farmers have discovered it was much easier to remain under the patronage of the state. As long as they received subsidies for some crops and were protected from foreign competitors for others, they saw no advantage to keeping costs down. Rather, if costs rose too high, they would agitate for bigger subsidies. The farmers quickly learned that their livelihood did not depend on farming well, or producing what the market needed, or producing it at prices the consumer could afford, as much as their ability to rally political support. Due to the wide dispersion of the farm population throughout the nation and their relative strength in the outerlying districts with disproportionately high representation in the Diet, they could mount the biggest lobbies in the country. This gained them support in the ruling Liberal Democratic Party which was used to great advantage.

The farmers were also encouraged by the solid backing of the Ministry of Agriculture, which not only channeled considerable assistance, but singlemindedly pursued a policy of increasing domestic production. While Japan has pleaded the case of free trade for its industries, those dealing with agriculture have constantly urged greater self-sufficiency. They warned about the dangers of being dependent on the outside world for food and tried to promote as many crops as possible locally. The incipient threat of trade interruptions was played up when there was a temporary shortage of soyabean or wheat. But the likelihood of Japan not being able to buy all it wanted on world markets was rather slim.

Alas, despite the enormous sums pumped into the agricultural sector, little was achieved. Japan was not only unable to become self-sufficient, its dependence grew rapidly and became more extensive than that of other advanced countries. For example, its grain self-sufficiency declined from 80 percent in 1960 to a mere 48 percent in 1990, while Britain and Germany significantly improved their situation.[7] Productivity, as noted, was ludicrously low and hardly improving. While farmers earned decent incomes and some became rich by selling land, ordinary citizens had nothing to show for the effort. The average Japanese family had to spend 25 percent of disposable income on food, while Americans only paid 17 percent—and that was after paying the highest subsidies in the world, nearly twice the level of other industrialized countries.[8] This made agricultural policy a relative disaster.

Defeat of the "Distribution Revolution"

Many foreigners assume that the Japanese distribution sector has been drastically streamlined over the past decades. This may be due to the many articles that have appeared on the "distribution revolution." Or the even more numerous stories about the heroes of this revolution, like Isao Nakauchi, who built one small shop into the nation's largest chain, Daiei. Then there are the equally impressive feats of Masatoshi Ito of Ito-Yokado, Seiji Tsutsumi of

Seibu and Seiyu, and Noboru Goto of Tokyu—to say nothing of the welcome news that Seven-Eleven was expanding at breakneck speed and might soon be followed by Toys 'R' Us.

In truth, it is nothing short of miraculous that these players could cut through the maze of distribution channels that make doing business in Japan extremely complicated for the Japanese as well as for foreigners.[9] It was because of the sector's very complexity that new techniques had to be introduced and new opportunities arose to grow vigorously in certain directions. But the success stories of some should not blind us to what is happening in the rest of the sector.

There have been many such "revolutions" in Japan that burned bravely and somehow just died out or were contained. We might remember that when Mitsukoshi, a leading department store, came into existence about three centuries ago, it was also revolutionary. Since then, the number of department stores has risen considerably, and they have become quite conventional. The more recent booms began with the supermarkets and Japan's own variation on that theme, the "superstores." But that was not all. There have been waves of chain stores, specialty stores, convenience stores, discount stores, "concept" stores, "box" stores, and others.[10]

For a while, it really looked as if the smaller, more old-fashioned retailers would disappear and "Mom-and-Pop" were slated for extinction. The public clamored for lower prices and the only stores that could compete were the larger, more efficient units. They introduced new merchandising techniques, updated the management systems, and trained their personnel better. They started using computers and labor-saving devices. They could purchase in much larger quantities, often directly from the supplier, and even took to importing. Some of them developed their own brand products. And the prices did come down . . . at first.

But, when it comes to cost, it is amazing how resilient a small outlet can be. Mom, and pop, and the kids, if they have no other source of earnings, will accept to make less money simply to keep alive. They don't care how many hours they work and overtime does not upset them. In fact, some hardly recognize any difference between private life and commercial activities. Their rental is usually cheaper when they are not simply running the store out of their own home. They also offer accessibility, living in the same neighborhood as the shoppers. If you compare that with recruitment of high school (and now college) grads, trouble in getting people to work long hours for anything but good salaries (and paid overtime), the cost of the gadgets used by modern management, and the astronomic rentals of large premises in choice locations, you see why the new units are not *so* competitive.

The real problem of the more modern units, however, is that they seem to be fighting with one another more than with the small retailers. Department stores sell more and more food and daily necessities to compete with the supermarkets. The superstores compete with the supermarkets and the department stores by adding leisure items, clothing, and some furniture. Popular items are on sale in large outlets and small ones. And the various units tend to concentrate in specific areas, with a superstore opening just opposite another and down the street from the department store. The customer has a broad choice and may visit them all a bit. But, when pressed for time or too lazy to go out, the neighborhood shop is the winner, especially if it also offers delivery service.

In this tight competitive situation, the more modern units found it increasingly difficult to make a profit based on greater sales capacity. Defensively, they also tended to offer more "service" to hold on to customers. And with it they began to lose one of their prime advantages . . . low price. At one time, department stores had sold on price. But they decided that the better path was to provide breadth of selection, elegance of environment, higher quality personnel, and other frills. The superstores, once regarded as low-price, mass-sales outlets also slipped into the same rut and began increasing margins. Even Akihabara, popular among tourists for its deep discounts, used the old trick of lifting list prices to make the discounts look bigger. As for the more exclusive boutiques, they raised prices as a matter of policy, the higher the price, the better the goods were supposed to be. So, if prices are not that much better, why buy there?

Thus, although the new merchandising units have grown, the limits are already in sight. Not only has the expansion slowed significantly, they had to contend with a "counter-revolutionary" offensive. Small retailers have done much to modernize and presently offer a wider assortment or use improved methods. But they have also resorted to political means of resisting change. This was possible for the simple reason that they were so numerous and had so much staff. The nation's *tofu* makers, rice merchants, grocers, and the like, mom and pop, and the employees, and their families, added up to a tremendous number of votes. They brought pressure to bear on the Liberal Democratic Party, and the other parties, and found considerable support. In an economy that is not strictly liberal, and where it is natural to protect one interest or another, they won out against the innovators. And there were few consumer interests to complain.

As of 1973, legislation was introduced to control the opening of new stores with a sales floor area over 1,500 square meters, later reduced to a more modest 500 square meters. To open such stores, superstore and supermarket chains had to obtain building and business permits from the authorities. And the authorities had to consult the local commercial activities coordination council, in which the small shopkeepers had a substantial voice. Although not always blocked, they usually had to accept compromises regarding size which hampered economies of scale. Other rules restricted business hours and sales over weekends. With this, the distribution "revolution" petered out. Will it be revitalized now that the Big Store Law is gone? Not as likely as many claim.

For the much touted distribution "revolution" was also hampered, just like every other transformation, by the incredible conservatism of the Japanese. They clamored for lower prices, but they also wanted convenient location, broad selection, luxurious surroundings, and, especially, personal service. They demanded at least a show of the honor and respect Japanese customers have been getting from mere shopkeepers for centuries already. They expected to enter any shop and have diffident sales personnel greet them, look after their needs, and carefully wrap their purchases. On occasion, they wished to be served at home rather than making the long trip to the store.

Moreover, as income increased, there was an interest in the exceptional, the unusual, the exotic, something that would make a person stand out or give a taste of luxury. Mass produced cheese, kitchen utensils, or canned food was all right, but clothing, or cosmetics, or leisure articles had to fit one's personality. It was essential to look just right and any number of boutiques, novelty shops, sporting goods stores, knick-knack corners, and the like sprang into existence for these very special people the consumers were becoming. This moved merchandising in the opposite direction from the earlier trends, away from the mass market and towards the personal. The urge for individuality and diversity resulted in a fragmentation of the market that saved some of the smaller units and allowed many more to arise.

So, here we are, entering the 1990s, and it could hardly be maintained that things have changed radically over the past few decades. Japan still has the largest, costliest, and most cumbersome distribution system among the advanced countries. Although its population is only half that of the United States, it has about as many retailers and more wholesalers. The average Japanese retail outlet serves 70 households as compared to 109 in Britain, 134 in America, and 179 in Germany. There are two people working in wholesale for every three in retail, which shows just how clogged the pipeline from maker, to wholesaler, to retailer, to purchaser can be.[11]

This rather extravagant use (or waste) of personnel has been criticized for decades already. Yet, although it is hard to believe, the situation has been getting worse. There are actually more stores and more employees than ever. For example, from 1968 to 1988, the number of wholesalers rose from 240,000 to 436,000, the number of retailers from 1,432,000 to 1,620,000, and the number of employees for both from 7,343,000 to 11,179,000[12] (see Table 5.2). Employment in the distribution sector managed to grow more rapidly than the total population and eventually accounted for one-tenth of the population and one-fifth of the labor force.

So much for the "distribution revolution." Today, in Japan, there are still far too many people tending shop instead of doing more useful or essential things. And these large numbers weigh heavily on the economy. They explain, among other things, why

Table 5.2

The Distribution "Revolution"

Outlets/Personnel	Number (thousands)			
	1958	**1968**	**1978**	**1988**
Wholesale Establishments	193	240	369	436
Wholesale Employees	1,551	2,697	3,673	4,328
Retail Establishments	1,245	1,432	1,674	1,620
Retail Employees	3,273	4,646	5,960	6,851
Distribution Employees	4,824	7,343	9,633	11,179

Source: Management & Coordination Agency, *Japan Statistical Yearbook.*

productivity is so low, a mere two-thirds of the U.S. level. They are also part of the answer as to why prices are so high in Japan. Naturally, with goods passing through so many hands, and each intermediary taking a cut, prices tend to rise. Some of this can be justified, in a sense, by the heavy costs of personnel, premises, and other overhead. But, in addition to being complex and complicated, the distribution system leaves room for market imperfections (like price-fixing and other questionable practices) between makers and distributors. No wonder products are so expensive in Japan, including those made locally. And, there is little hope for improvement soon. It will take another few "revolutions" for Japan to catch up.

From Old Services to New

Japan's leaders are firmly convinced that it will lead the world into the post-industrial, service-oriented society of the 21st century, perhaps treading on the U.S.'s heels or, in more optimistic moments, hoping to get ahead. The tertiary sector already contributes about as much of gross domestic product as most European countries and the gap with the U.S. is closing. But, as we already saw for distribution, that is only part of the story. It is still necessary for the service sector to be reasonably efficient and provide those services which are truly necessary.

It is not certain Japan can qualify under either heading. The tertiary sector, as noted, has been growing rapidly. It already provides 56 percent of GDP. But it uses some 59 percent of the labor force to do so—not an overly productive scenario. A closer look at the figures is even more disconcerting. Most of the growth has come from "miscellaneous" services, whose share of the total actually increased 50 percent since 1970 so that by 1990 it accounted for fully 37 percent of tertiary production. But employment grew much faster than turnover, so it has been losing productivity almost as fast as more efficient sectors like finance, insurance, real estate, transport, and communications have been gaining.[13]

So it is necessary, rather than just speaking of services, to distinguish different categories. First, you have some that serve the economy directly and are intimately related with business. Then come many other services, often listed as "miscellaneous," that serve the general needs of individuals. The third also helps individuals, but in another way, since they are more closely related to old age and welfare.

If Japan is to move resolutely into post-industrial society, it should be more concerned with the first category than the second. And it has shown considerable progress. One branch that has done particularly well is leasing. There has also been growth in software services and expertise. The number of computer centers has burgeoned. Business consultants have made their appearance and more law, accounting, and auditing firms have arisen. Advertising has expanded at an impressive pace. The latest boom is for "temps" or *haken-shain*, almost unheard of two decades back. Yet, despite all the progress, Japan still lags parts of Europe and especially the United States.

There are various reasons for the lag, the most important being "cultural." The Japanese company being a relatively closed and compact unit, it likes to impose its control on everything related to it. For reasons of prestige, or to inflate assets, it tends to purchase its own equipment and even today many Japanese companies buy what U.S. firms would doubtlessly only lease. Getting along with outside personnel is even harder. "Lifetime" employees are not used to dealing with newcomers or assigning them tasks. To the extent work is accomplished by small groups, an individual who comes briefly or irregularly is hard to integrate. Only for specific tasks, especially specialized ones, is the situation easier. Thus, companies no longer hesitate to employ a temporary bookkeeper, typist, or programmer. But calling in a lawyer or business consultant, to whom company "secrets" must be revealed, goes against the grain.

Thus, business-related services have been growing rapidly, but not as fast as person-related ones. This could be readily seen for any number of branches, whether eating or drinking establishments, sports or leisure centers, or cultural and educational institutes. Much of this was sparked by the arrival of new, Western fads, with Western companies often leading the way, from McDonald's hamburgers to Blockbuster videos. As per usual, these imports were copied or emulated by Japanese rivals. But, oddly enough, the new did not always drive out the old, and there has also been an explosion of *sushi* chains, pubs and bars of every sort, as well as the more scurrilous massage parlors and love hotels. That may explain why this sector has done so well. It also explains why it has remained so inefficient, since rather than fewer there were more establishments and more employees.

However, it is uncertain whether this growth can continue. It was fed by rising personal incomes, changing tastes and generous company expense accounts which resulted in one "boom" after the other. It seems unlikely that income will keep expanding as rapidly. Most of the fads and fashions have already been indulged, and even companies are slightly more parsimonious than before. Equally important, many establishments are directly or indirectly competitive. Either you eat a hamburger or *sushi*. Either you play golf or tennis. Either you dine out with your wife or frequent a hostess. They are therefore fighting for the consumer's money and there is just so much of it. Price wars could thus erupt, as some have already, and weaker establishments will be driven out of business.

Perhaps this would not be the worst thing. The number of establishments would finally be reduced, and perhaps, in so doing, rationalize the sector with more larger companies hopefully making better use of staff. If not, service productivity will remain exceptionally low by all standards but Japan's. Why this may just be wishful thinking is explained in the next section.

This brings us to the third category, one that has also grown but not commensurate with the needs. The Japanese population is aging rapidly, so much so that it will have the oldest population structure of the advanced world by the year 2020. With only three decades to go, it could be assumed that the government would push growth energetically. In fact, in the 1960s and 1970s, it did. Then it got alarmed by the price tag, with health expenditures rising from 5 to 7 percent of national income from 1970 to 1990.[14] So, during the 1980s, it did what it could to pare costs and avoid the same trap as Western countries where the level is already much higher.[15]

That may make sense administratively. But it does not in human terms. There is no way of turning back the clock and, if Japan will have tens of millions of aged people in the 21st century, it must do something about them. That is, if it is to remain a decent and humane society. Yet, there are not enough old age homes or other housing for the elderly, there are not enough nurses or doctors to care for them, and there is not enough equipment or know-how to handle age-related illnesses. Worse, there is not enough money to get what will be needed when it is needed. Nor is there much hope this will change. The ruling party is not subject to sufficient pressure from the elderly (as opposed to business interests) and young Japanese no longer want dirty, dangerous, or demanding jobs which must be filled.

Thus, if the service sector is supposed to be the springboard for a spectacular leap into the post-industrial society, Japan is liable to fall flat on its face. At best, this sector has been absorbing excess labor in order to make manufacturing more productive. But inadequate efforts have been made to develop the specific branches that can directly promote industrial growth and make the whole economy more dynamic. Services related to people have largely contributed to an often illusory improvement in the quality of life. And the public sector has yet to prepare suitably for the essential task of caring for the aged in this brave new world.

A Surfeit of Personnel

Japan is blessed with extremely courteous and helpful service and distribution establishments. They receive the customer with a bow, look after any needs most diligently, provide a pleasant atmosphere during his stay, and then follow up to maintain a good relationship. They are frequently rewarded with continued patronage. Japan is also blessed with very persistent and very successful salesmen. They will come singly or in groups, they will come once or a dozen times. And usually they end up making a sale.

In the tertiary sector, as its name implies, "service" is the most crucial element. No effort will be spared to make the customer feel that he is the center of everything. A prime example of this can be found in the department stores which carry on the proud traditions of Edo times. There is not only a very large staff, with more than enough salesgirls so that no customer will have to wait long, there are many assistant managers strutting around to see that everyone is looked after properly. There may be a place to leave the children and perhaps an art exhibit to while the time away. To make the customer feel like royalty, there is one young lady, dressed in a fancy uniform, to help him (or more likely, her) into the elevator, another to push the button and call out the floors, and a third to bow low over the escalator.

Stories abound about the hard work and devotion of the sales staff. One, told in many variations, refers to the eager young salesman who finds that a certain shop had already bought from the competitor but who nevertheless tries to win the client. If no one has time to talk to him, he sticks around to observe the shop. Perhaps he gets to know the shopkeeper's staff, or his wife who runs the cash register. He does his best to make friends with the family, even offering to take the little boy for a walk. He comes with gifts now and then. Finally, one day, impressed by his persistence, the shopkeeper agrees to see the product and, although he may not be thoroughly convinced of its value, he is very impressed by the earnestness and sincerity of the young salesman. Thus, he gives a trial order and the path is opened to bigger and better things.

All this is obviously done to increase sales. Almost as obviously, there seems to be a close correlation between the number of people used and the eagerness to increase sales. Thus, when things get bad, rather than cut back on staff, one will frequently hire yet more and the salesmen will be sent out more often. It is felt that there is a relationship between the amount of time physically spent with the customer and the amount sold. So the customer will find himself approached more often than ever. The number of salesgirls in a store or hostesses in a bar may increase as well. And they will put in more hours or make greater efforts than ever.

But there seems to be much less interest in, or even awareness of, the cost side of the equation. Providing the sort of "service" that is necessary is a very expensive proposition. First, it is essential to have the right premises, located in a suitable place and with the kind of decor that inspires confidence, promises comfort, or meets some other psychological need of the customer. The other basic requirement is to provide the staff. Since service implies proper treatment, it is usually necessary to hire more than just enough personnel. It is preferable that there be a bit more, once again to show the solidity of an establishment, to keep a constant eye on the customer so that he not be kept waiting, and to tend to his every need. In addition, the staff must be trained just right, show a proper demeanor, know how to fulfill its role with suitable humility. Premises and personnel are very costly requirements nowadays. And since not just any premises and not just any personnel will do, they are proportionately more costly than in many other countries.

The situation can be worse when it comes to sales personnel sent out to deal with, or to find, customers. For they will be making far more pointless visits than fruitful ones, having to try many potential customers before finding one that is even interested in what they have to sell. Having come to the customer, rather than the other way around, it is up to them to arouse an eagerness to buy. This is often a rather lengthy process and can involve numerous repeat visits. But, in Japan, once having sold a product, the relationship does not cease. The sales personnel must still return periodically. This is not only for the necessary after-sales service or repairs. Many salesmen make calls just to keep in the good graces of the customer, checking that there are no problems, coming by to deliver any refills in person, or just dropping in to say hello . . . and see if there is not something else they can sell.

In normal times, the amount of "service" is quite considerable. But it is nothing compared to what happens when business is slack or when there are too many goods in stock. Then the attempts at sales become frantic. More staff is taken on, people are switched from production or clerical tasks into sales. Often, rather than just send out individual salesmen, they are unleashed in teams of two and more. They increase the number of visits and the length of the stay. And they come bearing all sorts of gifts, many hardly of interest to the customer. Finally, they may actually go so far as to lower the price if the sale cannot be made any other way.

During this process, too much attention is paid to moving product, and not enough thought is given to related costs. The fact that so much personnel has to be used inflates the company's expenses. The fact that the personnel has to be well-trained, sometimes also well-educated, and know how to behave suitably, makes the wages of such personnel quite high, just below the industrial average for distribution, but well above it for services. If it is necessary, in times of surplus production, slow sales, or greater competition, to increase this already considerable cost, then something will give. It is possible that the company itself will find its profit margin getting slimmer and slimmer. Or it may shift some of the burden onto the consumer who will find prices inching up.

Neither side is really well-served by the present situation. The distribution and service industries are burdened with too much personnel. They repeatedly made efforts at rationalization and then fell back into the old trap of hiring more staff. Over the years, they have found it impossible to make major progress in cutting down on the use of personnel and thus productivity is low. Not only is it much lower than the more dynamic manufacturing sector. It is low compared with other countries and quite simply low considered in any rational terms.

Nevertheless, the consumers are equally guilty, for they impose this burden on the tertiary sector. They frequent department stores which they know are using more personnel than necessary because they find them more pleasant. They go out of their way to visit fancy boutiques or high class shops of all sorts even when they know the goods will be more expensive. On the other hand, many avoid discount shops as unreputable or refuse to go out of their way to visit places like Akihabara where they know the same goods can be obtained more cheaply just because the "service" is bad. Too many Japanese find it flatters their ego to be received as very select customers whose patronage is highly desired. The men who belong to exclusive key clubs, bars, and the like find it impossible to wean themselves from the craving for servility and the treatment that makes them feel every inch a VIP when they enter such establishments.

Far less comprehensively, Japanese businessmen still make purchases from their favorite salesmen, those they have known for years or to whom they have grown accustomed, whether their merchandise is better or not. There are still many buyers who fall for the tricks of the young salesmen making a show of exceptional sincerity or zeal. In this, they are hardly better than housewives who, knowing nothing whatsoever about the stock market, will buy shares in a company because they like chatting with the salesman.

Even the more business-related services are faced with the sort of problems that sellers of kimonos have known for centuries. They must also come frequently, see that everything is running well, bow low and apologize humbly if anything is wrong, and see that repairs are made instantly. The fact that this service personnel may be expensively trained personnel, rather than just merchants, is disregarded. Anyone caught up in the tertiary sector has to place human relations above all other concerns.

This has resulted in a cycle which some might term a vicious circle, but is clung to like a beneficial lifeline by the Japanese. To sell, one uses personnel; to sell more, faster, or at higher margins, one uses more personnel. Thus, there is always a tendency for prices to rise as well. If the opposite tack were taken, it is just as conceivable that the problems could be solved as well or better. By using less personnel, it would be possible to lower costs and, eventually, prices. By lowering prices, it would be possible for people to buy more cheaply, benefiting the consumers, and to buy in larger quantities, benefiting the distributors and producers. This is the cycle usually resorted to outside of Japan. It might just work in Japan, too.

Bloated Bureaucracy

Although in a capitalist economy they are only expected to play a supporting role, the bureaucrats began proliferating during the period of high growth when the country could afford it and social services were expanding. However, even as low growth set in and when it could least be afforded, the number of personnel in the various administrative bodies kept on rising. It has gradually assumed very considerable dimensions. By 1980, there were 1,199,000 national government employees, 3,167,000 local government employees, and 940,000 government-affiliated corporation employees.

More striking yet, even when the nation's private firms were forced to cut back on personnel and sometimes reduce or hold wages down, this movement was not carried over to those whose patriotism was counted on to run the state. There was a basic principle that state employees should enjoy a wage level equivalent to that in the private sector, and their wages were geared to that. But this ignored the aspects in which they were well ahead. The most prominent advantage, in an era of vanishing lifetime employment, was that they faced little chance of being dismissed and could stay on in one post or another almost indefinitely. Moreover, with larger severance payments and pensions, their total earnings were greater.

Whether this number of rather well paid people was really necessary to handle the tasks assigned them and what they were worth has been a major issue. Although there was relatively little complaint about the central administration's staff, it was clear that personnel on the prefectural and local levels had been expanding at a terrific pace and it also became known that they were earning about 7 percent more. This made little sense when one considers that the educational level of the central civil servants is much higher and the very functions of some of the prefectural and local ones were anything but essential. On the other hand, there have been a few categories that were understaffed, such as teachers and welfare workers.

Even when justified, there is room for doubt as to whether the civil service is making the best use of its employees. The "bureaucratic" mode of operation is obviously pushed to an extreme here. The candidates are taken in through educational background and tests, where things are done properly, and through personal connections with local politicians or bureaucrats, where they are not. But, although the degree of specialization has been increasing elsewhere, those chosen are still the generalists, at most with some legal course work. The fact that they then undergo a period of rotation, moving about from section to section, prevents further specialization. Promotion, ruled more rigidly by seniority, is even less likely to result in the best man making it to the top here than in business.

Moreover, anyone who has dealt with the bureaucracy knows, already from what can be witnessed, that the organization is not always rational or carefully integrated.[5] It is easy to get shunted from office to office before finding the right one, should it exist. Those in some of the offices seem to have little effective work and any number can be seen reading newspapers, chatting with one another, or having tea. Many seats are empty with their occupants off on uncertain duties. The flaws that could be compensated for by the zeal of officials in earlier days are more likely to be harmful now that few apply for patriotic reasons and most candidates really just want a secure job. Most unpleasant, a phenomenon rarely encountered in the private sector, there is a lack of courtesy toward the caller or applicant which is incomprehensible coming from a civil servant, namely someone paid for by the public to serve the public, but quite understandable coming from a "bureaucrat."

A major task of the bureaucracy seems to be producing forms to be filled in by the public. If all these forms are necessary, then there is little reason for complaint. But many businessmen (foreign and national) who have to deal with them find that the forms are unduly complicated and unduly numerous. Indeed, it often takes an expert to know how to fill in a form and the bureaucrats tend to get impatient with amateurs. This paper work which justifies their existence can have a deadening effect on those who get bogged down in the red tape. Although rules and regulations have not encroached as much on business as in the U.S., for example, many bureaucrats also live to fulfill regulations and the more the better, for them at least. This trend is not lacking and, if it were to continue, could easily get out of hand in a nation with a bureaucratic tradition as noble as Japan's.

The fact that the bureaucracy, especially at the lower levels, is not only a machine to accomplish specific tasks, but rather part of the general political process, means that it can become a center for brokerage as well. Civil servants are beset with requests from contractors for work, by pressure groups demanding services, and even by influential citizens seeking special favors. That all of them cannot be rejected is evident from the results. The bureaucrats give in most readily when politicians enter the scene and promote a specific project or request. Thus, various bodies are created that serve little useful purpose for the general public despite their great value to special interests. There are often more public works than strictly necessary or, rather, too many projects for those with political clout and too few for the rest. And the whole operation saddles the administration with additional staff it does not quite know how to use, although some job is always found.

This state of affairs was unpleasant, but bearable, during the period of rapid growth when Japan had a comparatively small government. However, as the economy slowed the government sector kept growing, thus creating an uncomfortable burden. Moreover, to the ordinary expenses of running the state were added increasing welfare costs. The share of national income absorbed by taxation and social security, which was kept under 20 percent during the 1960s, rose quickly toward 30 percent in the 1970s and 40 percent in the 1980s. Once lagging far behind the U.S. and Europe, Japan was rapidly catching up. With this, it clearly entered the age of "big government."

These trends worried some in the government. As far back as 1962, a committee was set up to promote administrative reform.[16] Successive cabinets came up with vague plans to streamline the constantly growing bureaucracy, most notably under Prime Ministers Miki and Fukuda. Prime Minister Ohira went yet further, making administrative reform a major plank in order to overcome the worsening financial crisis. Rather stringent proposals were put forward to cut costs and personnel. But nothing much came of this until the business community pressed for action. In 1982, Toshiwo Doko, former head of the Japan Federation of Economic Organizations (Keidanren) became chairman of the Second Ad Hoc Committee on Administrative Reform and warned then Prime Minister Suzuki that big business was tired of "big government."

This seemed to usher in a new era of belt-tightening. The committee recommended, among other things, a freeze on hiring, control of wages, decrease in subsidies, sale of land and assets, and reduction of public corporations, all this while maintaining proper levels of service through increased efficiency and productivity. The task of implementing these measures was entrusted in Yasuhiro Nakasone, who became prime minister in 1982. However, when he ran into other difficulties, his initial zeal waned. His successors, Prime Ministers Takeshita, Uno, and Kaifu were too busy with other matters, including serious scandals, to bear down on the bureaucracy. Thus, administrative reform petered out once again. Staffing had been cut somewhat, there were modest reductions in subsidies, two ministries were merged into one, and three major public corporations were sold, the national railways, telephone monopoly, and tobacco monopoly, although the debt from the first (about ¥30 trillion) more than wiped out the gains from the other two.

This was not much to show for so much effort. The bureaucracy was still too large, too costly, and too inefficient in the view of most citizens. And its intervention was increasingly resented by businessmen. No wonder Keidanren was dissatisfied with the results.

Despite eight years of reform, there appears to have been no fundamental change in the self-propagating nature of the administration or in conflicts among the various ministries and agencies over their jurisdiction. In fact, the reforms undertaken in the area of administration seem inadequate when compared with the efforts of private enterprise to improve efficiency.[17]

With so little accomplished by so many government and business campaigns, the pertinent question would appear to be "Why?" In Japan, to begin with, it is hard to dismiss staff and this is particularly true in the civil service where tenure is often guaranteed. Only by attrition, not hiring new people, can much be done. Yet, even this is hard to obtain and the various bodies have gone about increasing staff with impunity. This is largely because of the overly close relations between the politicians and bureaucrats. There is a tendency for local politicians to recommend their supporters to the local administrations which may hire them. The bureaucrats are no better, engaging in empire-building that would shock executives in private companies, and finding room for their own friends hired through connections. Some of the special agencies were also established either by LDP politicians as a means of obtaining campaign funds from those favored with contracts or by bureaucrats to provide retirement jobs.

In the central administration, it is even harder for the government to move the top bureaucrats to cut down on their own budgets or staff because it leans heavily on them in its day-to-day work. Moreover, the bureaucrats have their own special supporters among former bureaucrats who have entered the LDP or other parties. Even the socialist party would not be too keen on a reduction in personnel since the lower level staff, where unions are permitted, most often join leftist bodies. Nothing much can be done by the public to impose its wishes aside from showing a reluctance to pay more taxes, a mood that already prevails. But some of the local bodies have escaped even that constraint by floating bonds which have accumulated as perilously as the central government's own debt and will have to be paid by the taxpayers, or their children, in the future. ■

Notes

1. Economic Planning Agency.

2. Ministry of Labor, *Handbook of Labor Statistics*, annual.

3. Bank of Japan, *Comparative International Statistics*, annual.

4. For a comprehensive study of just how unproductive Japanese agriculture is, see Cornelius L.J. Van Der Meer and Saburo Yamada, *Japanese Agriculture: A Comparative Economic Analysis*.

5. *Japan Economic Journal*, April 20, 1991.

6. *The Economist*, June 1, 1991, pp. 31-32.

7. See Ministry of Agriculture, *White Paper on Agriculture*, annual.

8. *The Economist*, June 8, 1991.

9. On the complexity of the distribution system and how to use it nonetheless, see Michael Czinkota and Jon Woronoff, *Unlocking Japan's Markets*.

10. On the new merchandising possibilities, see Czinkota and Woronoff, op. cit., pp. 111-140.

11. See Randall S. James, "The Japanese Distribution System," *Journal of the ACCJ*, December 1987, pp. 46-54.

12. Management and Coordination Agency, *Japan Statistical Yearbook*, annual.

13. Economic Planning Agency.

14. See George J. Schieber and Jean-Pierre Poullier, "Overview of International Comparison of Health Care Expenditures," *Health Care Financing Review*, Annual Supplement, 1989, pp. 1-8.

15. Woronoff, *Politics, The Japanese Way*, pp. 287-297.

16. For more on administrative reform, see Woronoff, op. cit., pp. 291-302.

17. *KCC Brief No. 56*, Keizai Koho Center, June 1990.

6

Failings and Failures

Not Quite as Advertised

■ If this were a book on U.S., British, Chinese, etc., management, the following chapter would hardly be necessary. It would not be indispensable to dwell on which aspects of the management system have gone wrong in practice, why companies have made serious blunders, and just how poorly managers can do when they forget the basics. That sort of information is amply supplied in the professional literature and embroidered on in business newspapers and magazines.

Alas, for Japan, such material hardly exists in English. Almost everything you come across highlights the drive of one company or another, the brilliant plans (often just verbally expressed) of charismatic managers, and lurid explanations of how the Japanese outdid their many foreign rivals. True, now and then a company goes bankrupt or gets entangled in a political scandal. But such events are often glossed over or regarded as an aberration, an exception which proves the rule, when it may just as well be the rule that is wrong.

What is even sillier, some of our management gurus do not even realize that somebody's success may be someone else's failure. Thus, Pascale and Athos trumpet the great success of Matsushita, barely mentioning that it was at the expense of numerous other Japanese companies.[1] Or James Abegglen, who should know better, gives a blow-by-blow description of how Honda beat Yamaha for motorcycles.[2] This shows Honda's exceptional ability. Doesn't it also reveal some inability of Yamaha, which is no less Japanese?

It is only by demonstrating, through more negative interpretations and unflattering examples, that there are serious flaws in Japanese companies, among Japanese managers, and in Japanese management as such, that outsiders can begin to understand the situation. This description is much longer than anything that has appeared in the literature so far. Yet, it is just the tip of the iceberg. There were many more mistakes, blunders, and muck-ups—that much can be realized by anyone who follows the Japanese scene or has actually done business in Japan. Still, it will have to do for now and until the foreign coverage of Japanese management becomes more balanced, objective, and similar to coverage of everybody else's foibles or as revealing as the Japanese media's coverage of their own system.

The purpose is obviously not to induce smugness among foreigners when they realize that Japanese companies are not quite as good as they are supposed to be. After all, there are plenty of capable ones and you have to watch out for them. But, for the time being, smugness is less of a threat than the nervousness and anxiety that strike many foreign managers when confronting the Japanese. They really do think they are facing exceptional beings they cannot possibly vanquish. So it does not hurt to cut the Japanese down to realistic size. And remember, if they appear to be doing something foolish, this may not be a trick or ploy but a genuine mistake.

Even more important, as will be stressed further on, the best way to beat the Japanese is to take advantage of their weaknesses and failings. To do so, of course, you must know them better. This presentation should contribute to that knowledge.

The Big Picture

At this point, some readers may wonder why—if there are so many failings in Japanese management—are the Japanese doing so well? The answer is quite simple. No matter how good things may look from the outside, they are nowhere near as impressive when seen from within. The various failings have had a definite negative effect on Japanese business and the economy more generally. Indeed, they are serious enough for Japanese managers to wonder whether the system should not be reformed.

One reason why the failures are not as evident to outsiders is perspective. Foreigners tend to see largely the more dynamic sectors and more aggressive companies and ignore the rest. They also tend to compare things to the situation in their own country, whose weaknesses are more familiar and more pressing. Finally, part of the fault lies with those who write on Japanese management, whether academics or journalists, and who are keener on telling a rousing success story than a boring tale of mishaps.

To clear away some misconceptions, let's start with the plausible idea that the Japanese economy is strong, *thus* managers must be doing the right things. Yes, the economy is still more robust than most Western ones (although it has clearly fallen behind other Asian countries). But, as noted earlier, it is slowing markedly. Couldn't that just as well be traced to less talented or dynamic managers who are still following policies that made more sense in the 1960s and 1970s than in the 1980s and 1990s?

Something similar has happened to productivity. Manufacturing productivity improved rapidly in the 1960s and 1970s, but has slackened since. Naturally, part of the sluggishness can be traced to maturity. But there is another aspect. The best progress was made when new machinery, more advanced technologies, and larger scales could be introduced. Now that it has become necessary to apply more creative techniques, Japanese managers don't seem to be doing so much better than their Western counterparts.

What is worse, while Japan has been in front for manufacturing productivity, it has been in the rear in just about every other sector. It has done poorly in agriculture, mining, construction, distribution, and services. These are all areas which employ large numbers of personnel and where the biggest productivity gains come from working smarter, not harder. Yet, Japan has not come up with very many bright ideas. If anything, it has proven unusually profligate in the use of people.

So, it is possible that foreigners have not seen Japan's failures because they were not looking in the right places. For one, there was no shortage of difficulties in the various declining industries, from textiles, to ships, to petrochemicals, and even to steel. And they were even less tractable outside of manufacturing. That is, if you will remember, the bulk of the economy. Similarly, foreigners did not bother looking at the smaller companies which happen to account for 99 percent of all companies. If they had taken an occasional glance there they would have realized that something was wrong.

First of all, smaller companies are less capitalized, which means that they cannot buy enough machinery and acquire the more advanced technologies needed to keep going. Whenever the economy turns down, they are the first to be deprived of loans and, lacking their own financial resources, they are also the first to run out of money. Now, along with financial and technological weakness, it is necessary to add staffing. Small companies have always gotten whatever workers were left over, the less educated, less skilled, less loyal. But, with tightness in the labor supply and increasing dislike of dirty, dangerous, and demanding jobs, they frequently cannot find anyone and must close shop.

The situation is particularly bad for subcontractors because they do not even have direct access to work. They accept whatever jobs their "parent" company offers. In good times, such work may abound. In poor times, it dries up very quickly. What is more, the parent company tends to take in some of the jobs it formerly subcontracted in order to keep its own staff busy. This means that a large portion of the "success" of big companies can be explained by the "failure" of small ones. This is not the noblest way of keeping ahead, but a very widespread one, to judge by the comments of a subcontractor who explained how Japan's major companies got through the heavy yen (*endaka*) crisis so well.

The answer is clear to anyone who ever studied Japanese business seriously. The big companies pretended to tighten their belts. Many put out idiotic press releases about how they were saving scraps of note paper or using pencils down to their stubs to save money. But it was all a sham. The real savings were achieved the old-fashioned way: the companies ordered their smaller subcontractors to cut prices. As the yen appreciated, they simply ordered more price cuts—and then more again. Yes, a lot of small companies went out of business. But what is that compared to the preservation of the Japanese economy? The large companies are the backbone of industry, or so the large companies insist.

They must survive at all costs, they say. And survive they did.[3]

While foreigners were hardly aware of the trials and tribulations of backward firms or small subcontractors, it is amazing that there was not more notice of another group of companies which had been wildly applauded during the early 1980s. This was the batch of venture-capital firms that were highly innovative and rapidly expanding. They were expected to galvanize the economy and grow into the Sonys and Hondas of the 1990s. Alas, most of them disappeared within a decade of being founded, including such stars as SORD Computer and the robot-maker Dainichi Kiko. They could not penetrate the domestic market, they could not get enough funds, and they were eventually squeezed out or bought up by bigger players.

Thus, there have been plenty of failures in Japan. In some cases, they resulted in the demise of the company which filed for bankruptcy. This has been cyclical. In 1984, the number of bankruptcies rose to 26,000, only to fall back thereafter and reach a low of 10,000 in 1989. Since then, however, the trend has again been upward and may continue if the yen remains strong and a recession strikes. Moreover, although the number of bankruptcies has declined, the value of outstanding debts continued growing. By 1991, it reached a peak of more than ¥6 trillion.

Yet, the number of actual bankruptcies is even less symptomatic than another trend. Year after year, the National Tax Administration has announced that about half of all Japanese companies reported losses . . . not profits. Admittedly, one cannot entirely trust their figures and they may have stashed some money aside. But it is clear that many companies are not adequately profitable and some are just kept going because they provide a job for the owners. Others are probably defunct but nobody bothered dissolving the firm formally.

Of course, most of these are smaller companies. But the situation for larger enterprises is not particularly rosy. According to a study by the Japan Development Bank, for the 1,000 manufacturers it surveyed, the ratio of operating profits to sales dropped from 9.3 percent in 1969 to 3.5 percent in 1987. A similar, long-term decline occurred for operating profits as a percentage of assets, peaking at 10 percent in 1969 and sinking to 5 percent in 1987.[4] While Japanese managers do not stress profits, and usually are less profitable than foreign counterparts, this shows that even in their own terms the situation has been steadily deteriorating.

Mismanaging Japanese-Style

All too often, the Japanese management system is presented in the abstract and it is simply assumed that the Japanese apply it properly. Is that a safe assumption? Just as Western managers can mismanage their companies even when going by the book, Japanese managers who have spent their whole career in the same corporate culture can make serious mistakes. Indeed, in certain ways the management system itself encourages widespread abuses.

Some of the most serious problems derive from the practice of rotation, where staff in general, and especially those who will eventually hold managerial positions, are moved from job to job over the years. Despite the advantages of knowing more jobs and more people, there are definite drawbacks. One is that rotation is too frequent. It occurs every two or three years. This means that employees are not in any job long enough to learn it well. Indeed, during the initial period they are just finding their way around and, as the next rotation approaches, they tend to lose interest. So, they are only active and able in the middle portion while the rest is wasted.

In addition, rotation is frequently quite erratic. It is not carefully designed as a learning process whereby individuals move about to related jobs. Thus, even in trading companies it rarely happens that an employee will be posted to Dahomey and later France, both French-speaking countries, or from steel to an allied sector like shipbuilding. No, the transfer is as likely to be from Dahomey to Brazil, so any French acquired is wasted, or from steel to computer software. Indeed, it frequently appears to those concerned that they are assigned to fill whatever seat becomes vacant with little thought to the matter. This type of randomness does not boost morale.

Another underlying principle, which the Japanese apparently believe, is that employees should be able to handle every kind of task. Thus, they are shifted from sales, to personnel, or to public relations with scant concern as to their earlier training, innate abilities, or personal wishes. Even research and development receives generalists. In many cases, you end up with the proverbial square peg in a round hole, someone who cannot do the job. Equally bad, should you find someone ideally suited to that job, namely a round peg, it is almost certain that come the next rotation he will be put in another hole, perhaps a square one.

This generates an enormous amount of inefficiency and incompetence which is further accentuated by the career escalator. For many years after they are hired, all employees rise at the same pace, whether they are more or less capable. So it is not surprising that incompetent managers should proliferate, much to the annoyance of more talented or diligent underlings who have to do the work for them without much reward. This generates frustration, especially among those who show ability or drive and want to rise faster. Realizing this, Toyota recently demoted about 1,000 middle-managers to lower-level jobs. Were their juniors upset? Not to judge by this reaction: "Before, the *kacho* just gave instructions, from now on we can ask him to move the pencil a bit, too."[5]

Only at higher levels, including top posts, is seniority no longer a major criterion. There it is supposedly ability that counts. Yet, when ability has been systematically ignored at all lower levels and the better elements discouraged from stepping out of line, how is it possible to judge ability? As in so many other bureaucratized institutions, the Japanese company is more likely to promote yes-men and flunkies who have kept on good terms with their bosses. Problems thus arise in two respects. The younger managers may not be as smart or tough as the older ones. Also, in larger companies, they may have formed factions that vie for power.

Even the highly praised practice of bottom-up management does not work out as nicely in practice as in theory. For the theory, here is Vogel's description:

> The lowly section, within its sphere, does not await executive orders but takes the initiative. It identifies problems, gathers information, consults with relevant parts of the company, calls issues to the attention of higher officials, and draws up documents. Of course, the section acts within the context of the wishes of higher officials and is in constant communication with them. . . . Good decisions emerge not from brilliant presentations of alternatives but from section people discussing all aspects of the question over and over. . . .[6]

With regard to practice, there are several prominent drawbacks. For one, there can be so many individuals in on the decision-making process that it is extremely hard to get them to agree on anything. Thus, the question is discussed over, and over, and over, and over. . . . This was one of the gripes of Honda's new chief executive, Nobuhiko Kawamoto:

> We'd get the people from research, sales and production together and everyone would say 'not this' and 'not

that.' We'd talk, but there would be no agreement. . . . Product planning has to be on a tight schedule. But we'd have another discussion, and another study and then more preparation. And finally, the decision would come months later.[7]

This business of going round and round affected not only Honda, which is actually one of the more actively managed concerns. It occurred everywhere. And the next hurdle was that, once a decision had been reached further down, it was still necessary to get everyone above to sign on. This involved further delays, especially if there were too many layers of management. Toyota, despite its use of lean production, was recently dismayed to realize that it was top-heavy. Ideas had to be approved by no less than seven superiors, each of whom had to affix his personal *hanko* (seal) of approval. The result, according to Atsumi Kamano, general personnel manager, was a severe case of "big-corporation disease, where people just do what they are told to do." If this afflicted Japan's foremost automaker, how much worse must things be in even more bureaucratized companies.[8]

As for the *ringisho* themselves, the primeval source of many decisions, they are not without flaws. Even one of the stronger supporters of the practice, Mitsubishi's Shunzo Arai, conceded that:

> Anybody with an idea puts it on a *ringisho*. Anybody with pride wants to be on its circulation list. The result is a ritual dance of circulating and approving that has nothing whatsoever to do with meaningful work. The *ringisho* certainly deserves criticism. I think the Japanese would greatly benefit by reducing the complexity and formality of the *ringi* system, while preserving its undoubtedly good features.[9]

Aside from the risk of nothing getting done, bottom-up management occasionally entails the risk of the wrong things getting done. By letting lower level personnel take decisions, their activities can go contrary to general company policy. Indeed, they may just take the ball and run without reflecting on whether they are moving in the same direction as everyone else. That occurs where controls are too weak or leaders put too much faith in the ability of lower level staff to do the right thing. That has been seen in many recent cases of criminal wrongdoing in banks and securities firms. The urge of the natural resources division to launch a major oil project resulted in the collapse of the trading company Ataka. C. Itoh was only saved from a similar fate when a new president dropped its oil subsidiary. And Itoman lost heavily on land speculation which was not strictly its line of business.

Equally interesting is what happened recently to Sanrio, famous throughout Japan for its novelty characters, when it decided to open a theme park. This task was entrusted to a special team, which was to design and operate the park. Left too much leeway, it went on a building and hiring binge, far exceeding the original budget. Worse, rather than use Sanrio's existing characters, they invented their own. That was like running Disneyland without Mickey Mouse. By then, the president, who had previously stuck to his motto of "when you tell someone to do a job, let him finish it," had had enough and intervened.[10]

The worst consequence of bottom-up management, however, may be how it affects top management. It becomes uncommonly difficult for company executives to coordinate the activities of the various divisions and impart any clear direction. Once that was not as serious because many of the early postwar business leaders were entrepreneurs or strong personalities who knew how to guide, inspire or manipulate the rest of the staff. Now that they are going, often their successors will find it hard to lead even when they want to. Worse, more and more of these supposed "leaders" are not even interested in doing that, they would rather "cover their asses" to put it bluntly.

Thus, bottom-up management becomes the ideal way for company executives to let others assume the responsibility of proposing and adopting decisions. If the resulting action is wise, they will share in the glory. If it is foolish, there is somebody else to blame it on. Or, in typical Japanese fashion, they will see what other companies are doing and let them take the lead. Again, if they are right, fine. If they are wrong, well you cannot be blamed for doing the same thing as your competitors, can you?

That may be why so many once dynamic companies are now looking rather drab, including Nissan, Honda, even Toyota, Matsushita, Seibu Saison, and others mentioned in this respect. As indicated, a lot of the trouble resides at the top. And an increasing number of companies have become dissatisfied with those leading them, although it is rarely made public until the boss is sacked. The reasons are, oddly enough, at both extremes. Some, like Shigeru Okada of Mitsukoshi and Suemitsu Ito of Itoman, were regarded as too "bossy." But most were actually too weak, especially those unfortunate souls called upon to replace the company's founder. The most striking example was Matsushita, whose hand-picked successor was later eased out. Honda also went through assorted reshuffles to end up with an "emergency troika." This betrays a definite crisis of leadership in a society where "leading" is not highly evaluated.

As can be seen, like any other management system, there is usually a logic to how things go wrong. That is why, some time back, I devised Woronoff's laws of Japanese management which are no more facetious or less useful than Parkinson's laws when considering American management.[11] Here are some examples.

1. Like the Peter Principle, many Japanese will rise to the level of their incompetence because the career escalator takes them further than they could get on the basis of

ability. So don't be surprised if you encounter many incompetents. The corollary is that if things are running well anyway, there must be people further down who are covering for them. A practical tip: seek them out and cultivate them.

2. At lower levels, there will also be many incompetents. That is because, with rapid rotation, some will not have had time to learn the ropes while others are preparing to leave. The most useful staff are probably in their second year.

3. Even in specialized positions, there are many amateurs because staff is often allocated with little attention to special training, experience, or inclination. You may actually know more than most of them.

4. It will take longer than elsewhere for decisions to be reached, due to meetings and *nemawashi*. And, contrary to rumor, action will not be much faster because it will involve many other decisions.

5. Consensus does not mean so much that everyone agrees but that opponents are tired of disagreeing. It expresses support by those who like the policy and something quite different from those who dislike the policy and want the originators to get in trouble.

6. When too many companies agree on the same thing, they are probably wrong. With everyone jumping on the same bandwagon, even good ideas will have bad results due to overproduction, underpricing, and excessive competition in general.

7. With frequent rotation at the base and reshuffles at the top, there is no true long-term policy so much as many small segments that add up, because it is so hard to

change direction. If change comes, it is less likely to derive from new ideas than new people. Another practical tip: never forget to cultivate the juniors of your counterparts for one day they will take charge.

Even Japanese Make Mistakes

Whether resulting from a bottom-up or top-down approach, decisions made by Japan's companies are not always the wisest. Like managers everywhere, the Japanese make mistakes and sometimes quite disastrous ones. The only difference is that they keep them secret better than most and, due to dispersed decision-making, it is harder to pin the blame on any given person. Still, from scanning the business press, enough fiascos can be found to show cause and effect.

Obviously, there have been countless troubles in the declining sectors such as textiles, garments, shipbuilding, shipping, coal, aluminum, and even steel. Thousands of companies have gone under and more should follow. But putting the blame solely on the industry's decline would be incorrect. In each cases, the Japanese expanded much too far and created unpardonable excess capacity, often due to official targeting policy.[12] This means that more facilities had to be closed and more companies were ruined than otherwise. Not having learned from past lessons, we can encounter the same thing even in today's flourishing industries when they overproduce, such as with consumer electronics, semiconductors or computers.

One particularly poignant example is the fierce—and destructive—competition over dynamic random access memory chips (DRAMs). Each time a new generation was developed, makers immediately expanded production in order to claim a larger market share. Alas, supply soon outstripped demand and prices plummeted. Yet, without having learned their lessons, makers promptly geared up for the next round. This happened for the 1K chips, then the 4K, then the 16K, then the 64K, and on to 1M, 4M and beyond. What was the result? Modest profits for some. Losses for others. And an industry in which, according to NEC senior managing director Hajime Sasaki, "the way things are now, no one will be able to make any money from DRAMs."[13]

Suffering through a recession or sectoral decline is one thing, reacting unwisely and expanding when one should cut back is another. In the early 1980s, this occurred with Sanko Steamship, once the world's largest tanker operator. Sanko wagered that the price for building new ships had touched bottom and charter rates would rise. It therefore ordered huge numbers of ships to benefit from this expected upturn. When the market did not recover it was stuck with empty ships. The outcome was the biggest bankruptcy ever with over ¥1 trillion in debts. Sanko was not the only one affected, this glut hurt all shippers and even the venerable Japan Line sought rehabilitation.

Any company that is in a declining or stagnant sector should realize that it must either retrench or seek other opportunities through diversification. Many of the firms which have since disappeared failed to diversify, and little need be said of them. More worrisome are those which diversified foolishly, and they are legion. Seibu Saison is a case in point. It rushed headlong into one project after the next, expanding its empire to include dozens of ventures in distribution, transport, leisure, and services. There were so many, in fact, that management could not control the lot and some turned out to be duds.

But it was no exception. Diversification became a passion, and a panacea, in corporate circles. Just take the steelmakers. The six biggest firms set up over 500 new ventures in three years in the late 1980s.[14] Some were close to home, like making oil rigs or turn-key plants, others more remote. They included videotape materials, assorted electronic goods, semiconductors, silicon and other new materials, and biotechnology. Most popular, since they had land, was to open hotels and theme parks.

It did not take long to realize that many of these ventures had been a mistake from the start. The steelmakers were newcomers who lacked technological know-how, skilled personnel, and suitable facilities. They also lacked the marketing capability and distribution network. For the hotels and theme parks, location was often wrong in addition. Aside from that, with so many newcomers pushing into already crowded sectors, capacity grew immensely, margins were squeezed, and all the players were hurt financially. Thus, the launchings were followed by liquidations.

On the receiving end, the epitome of the diversification fad was biotechnology. It attracted countless entrants from everywhere. Not only pharmaceuticals, which at least had the background and personnel, but chemicals, textiles, beverages, and general manufacturing. After all, biotechnology was the industry of the future. Unfortunately, all too many managers forget that it might take years of painstaking research to come up with new products and promote them. The pay-off would be very long in coming. Apparently not all could wait despite a supposed penchant for "investing for the long term."

Investing for the long term, allied with the urge for bigness and craving for overseas expansion also caused many Japanese firms to make huge, terribly risky bets which might—or might not—pay off. This included Bridgestone's $2.6 billion acquisition of Firestone. It was seen as essential to become a top world producer, but the price was clearly inflated and Bridgestone had to follow up with $1.5 billion to rationalize and modernize the facilities it bought, which were overstaffed and technologically outdated. The initial impact was certainly negative, a drag on profits.

Even riskier were Sony's acquisition of Columbia for $3.4 billion and Matushita's purchase of MCA for $6.6 billion. There is cause to question the rationale, namely that hardware producers should expand into software to benefit from conceivable synergies. More worrisome is that, unlike a tire factory, it is difficult to project how well a film studio will do in the future. Additionally, this type of artistic endeavor is far removed managerially from producing electronics. It was also uncertain just how well Japanese could manage large numbers of Americans. At any rate, it could be argued that Sony paid too much for Columbia, 200 times earnings as opposed to Matsushita's 34 times for MCA.[15] On the other hand, it is possible that Matsushita's decision had less to do with logic and more to do with outpacing Sony.

Whether it is fear of "losing face," investing for the long term or, more commonly, inability to assess value or haggle over prices, the Japanese have repeatedly paid top dollar, top mark, and top franc to obtain what they wanted. This applied to the Bridgestone and Sony acquisitions. It also applied to the wild binge in the late 1980s when Japanese developers bought up golf courses, hotels, and other prime real estate around the world. Within years, the real estate market weakened and, on paper at least, they had lost a fifth or a quarter of their value. Of course, one day prices would go up and the Japanese might realize a profit.

While some of the errors indicated above seem ordinary, almost inevitable given Japanese business practices, it is more surprising to discover that many companies got into trouble because of inadequate technology. Yet, Mazda was almost ruined by the boss' predilection for the rotary engine, which was never perfected and furthermore unattractive because it consumed too much fuel. Honda was stymied in the late 1960s because its founder preferred air-cooled to water-cooled engines. Indeed, even companies which continually came up with brilliant innovations, like Victor Company of Japan (JVC), could run out of good ideas. It was stuck with nothing to replace its video-cassette recorders. More fatal was Riccar, once the top sewing machine manufacturer, which failed to introduce automated, electronic models in time.

However, the biggest share of debacles recently can be traced to what would at first appear to be most un-Japanese behavior. The Japanese tirelessly lecture foreign businessmen about the need to concentrate on the core business, devote more funds to research, and avoid money games. Yet, time and time again, Japanese companies have gone under or been severely hurt by investments in land, and lately art, or the purest of financial punts.

In the early 1990s, many companies were hit by the slump in land and property prices following the extraordinary boom of the late 1980s. By the way, this was not the first time it happened, other firms were caught out by Tanaka's plan to rebuild the archipelago when they bought land slated for developments which never came. The big loser then was Kojin, a textile firm. In this new batch of losers, some were developers, like Nanatomi which became the nation's third largest bankruptcy. But trading companies also invested unwisely, Itoman being notable here. And the banks had loaned the investors too much, which is why Heiwa Sogo had to be rescued by Sumitomo Bank.

More surprising than speculation in local property was the sudden appearance of Japanese as art collectors, snatching up the most expensive paintings in the world and bidding for every old master that came on the market. In 1990 alone, they spent ¥490 billion on 1.5 million paintings and art objects. This was done with little past experience or love of art, often just to show that they had "arrived." One of the foremost was Ryoei Saito, whose paper company Daishowa became deeply indebted for a second time. By the way, Itoman also dabbled in art, as did the chief executives of many blue chip companies. Alas, when prices fell, they had a lot of explaining to do.

Yet, nothing was quite as incredible as the craze for stock market investment (and speculation) which gripped not only individuals but supposedly sober companies during the 1980s. This formidable fad was known as *zaiteku*, namely the technology of using money to make money.[16] With this, managers used company funds to invest in the stock market and then plowed any earnings into further punts. At its peak, more than half the listed companies were engaging in *zaiteku* and they were a virtual who's who of Japanese industry including Toyota, Matsushita, Nissan, Sony, Honda, Mitsubishi, etc. Meanwhile, banks and brokers were busy financing investors and speculators, including some rather dubious ones.

Obviously, this is not how company money should be used. Rather, improving equipment, expanding plant, supporting R&D, raising wages, and other types of activities are generally expected of management. But managers continued to invest heavily in the market instead of in their companies. And prices rose regularly, partly because so much money was being pumped into the market. But, one day prices had to fall and the situation became quite different. Some of the players were seriously damaged. Tateho had already gone broke in 1987. Most managed to get by because they had other sources of earnings, although unrealized stock losses weighed heavily on the balance sheets of many companies and the banks or brokers which loaned most heavily to investors.

This brings us to the very last, and nastiest, category of business blunders, that is corruption or, more exactly, getting caught. For this can result in a scandal that tarnishes one's image or worse. One of the more memorable involved Prime Minister Tanaka, who talked Japanese airlines and the military into buying the right planes.[17] The Recruit scandal, which brought down one prime minister and sullied several others, resulted from insider trading by an up-and-coming businessman. The latest, and in some ways messiest, scandal involved all the major and many minor securities firms which compensated losses of some of their *zaiteku* clients.[18]

While compensating clients for stock losses was not illegal, other scandals were clearly more criminal in nature. Most unsettling recently was the discovery that four banks, including major ones, had issued forged certificates of deposit to other financial institutions. The amounts involved were significant, nearly ¥1 trillion in all. This was done by lower level personnel, often branch managers.[19] Meanwhile, further up, top executives of the trading house Itoman were charged with buying art works for the company at inflated prices and, nastier yet, embezzling company money to acquire company stock. This would seem to indicate, at the very least, exceedingly lax supervision and sloppy management.

This sketch of mistakes and failures is anything but complete. There are plenty of other examples for each category, with new ones arising all the time. But there are even more which never come to light. It is often only when a blunder is so serious that it creates a scandal or results in a bankruptcy or substantial losses that it is noticed. Otherwise, it is usually kept secret and covered up by the company to maintain face. This is bad enough. More worrisome is that, when they are caught, companies just sacrifice one or two executives who formally apologize or resign while the deeper causes go uncorrected. Thus, we can expect more of the same in the years to come.

Winners or Losers?

Odd as it may seem, the best way of concluding this section on failings and failures is to look at some of the supposed "success stories." That is, companies which in the West pass for successes although the evaluation in Japan can be quite different. Those featured here are Honda, Sony and Victor Company of Japan (JVC). But what applies to them applies more broadly in Japan's very different business environment. This should raise some interesting questions as to just what is meant by "good management."

Let's start with Honda. Founded just after the war by an engineer, it has maintained a passion for technological excellence. Soichiro Honda was a person who cared for his workers. He remarked that one capable man could perform the work of 10 or even 100 mediocre employees. Staff members were given more initiative and encouragement than elsewhere. Honda was also more adventuresome, among the first to export and then establish production facilities abroad. Meanwhile, it turned out a constant stream of good, reliable, reasonably priced cars and motorcycles. This was rewarded abroad. Sales rose steadily and it did far better than its Japanese rivals.

Back home, things were quite different in the automobile sector. Honda did advance and actually copped the third position for market share. Yet, all this while, first place was held by Toyota, which grabbed more and more market share while Honda's share stagnated.[20] Surely, Toyota was also ably run, it was careful about quality, it provided good service. Its workers were "motivated," as they say, but it was apparently the least popular automaker to work for. Aside from that, as everybody knew, Toyota was the most conservative maker. It was the last to venture abroad. Also, it was "always the last to make model changes and the last to take advantage of product innovation."[21]

Why did Toyota do so well in Japan (even if less brilliantly abroad)? There are various explanations. One is that it was the richest maker and could afford to ride out financial difficulties or even create them, knowing its competitors could not resist. It was more keen on market share than any other, officially setting the goal of 50 percent of domestic sales and 10 percent worldwide while knowing this meant others had to lose. Far more important, it had the biggest distribution network, five times the size of Honda's, and its salesmen could push more cars. Last but not least, since it was a follower, it could check that any innovations were successful before introducing them.

For motorcycles, the shoe was on the other foot. Honda was larger (thanks to its automobile division), it was richer, and it had the best distribution network. Thus, if rivals tried to expand their market share, it reacted vigorously. In the early 1980s, there was an epic battle between Honda and Yamaha, which sought to pull ahead. Yamaha greatly expanded production, introduced more new models than ever, and slashed prices. Honda responded by unveiling one model after the other and cutting its own prices. The result was gross overproduction, even by Japanese standards, and masses of unsold units.

In the end, Yamaha gave in and Honda had won the "HY war." This was presented by Abegglen and Stalk as a great achievement for Honda.[22] A more balanced view would regard it as a disaster all around, with all makers stuck with excess capacity, unsold inventory, and smaller profits or bigger losses. This hurt Honda as well since it could not defend itself in the automobile sector and saw its share slump. Indeed, it eventually sank to fourth position, behind Mitsubishi—the least imaginative, versatile, and dynamic maker but one with ample funds, good distribution, and support of a major *keiretsu.*

The scenario was rather similar for Sony. Established after the war by daring and creative leaders, it always placed great stress on technology. For electronics, a technology-led industry, this would seem essential. And Sony came out with one stunning product after another, the transistor radio, Trinitron picture tube, Walkman, and video cassette recorder. All the while, Akio Morita urged on his staff and gave them about as much leeway as can be expected in Japan. Personally rather affable and outspoken, he became the darling of the foreign business media.[23] And, in the U.S. and Europe, Sony was an enormous success.

Meanwhile, back in Japan, Sony enjoyed a considerably lower status and never managed to accumulate as much market share as its products deserved. It was regularly overshadowed by Matsushita, better known abroad for the National and Panasonic brands. Konosuke Matsushita placed his strongest emphasis on marketing.[24] He painstakingly built up a vast network of dependent outlets which he used to flog his products. And he arranged to produce virtually everything. How? By inventing them? No. He left that to others.

Matsushita's research laboratories kept a close watch on everything that was being produced by everyone else and how they were selling. Any new hits were quickly reproduced. With excellent production techniques, and not having had to waste money on creative R&D, it was then able to come out with something a bit better for a bit less. This was called "followership" by Pascale and Athos, who seem to think it was a very clever strategy, indeed. "From the outset, Matsushita rarely originates a product, but always succeeds in manufacturing it for less and marketing it best."[25] The Japanese themselves were not quite as flattering. Using a play on the Japanese verb *maneru* meaning to imitate, they gave Matsushita the nickname of "*Maneshita*."

It was the imitator or copycat and not the innovator which regularly gained the largest market share, thanks to its distribution capability and financial clout. Thus, Sony and the others only had a few years—and sometimes only a few months—to profit from their ingenuity before Matsushita moved in massively to conquer and saturate the markets. The key battle involved the video cassette recorder, which Matsushita licensed from JVC. It was pushed so hard that the VHS system drove Sony's Beta system into oblivion, although the latter was widely regarded as technologically superior.

There is one last chapter to this saga, it involves Victor Corporation of Japan. JVC was also a pioneer in television, stereo records, and video cassette recorders. Alas, unlike Sony, it was not independent but dependent on Matsushita, which owned 52 percent. It had to license its new products to Matsushita which often turned out to be its stiffest competitor. Since it had greater manufacturing capability, more captive outlets, and deeper pockets, it was actually Matsushita which cashed in most on JVC's inventiveness. By the 1990s, this was getting rather serious since JVC could only keep ahead by constantly introducing new products . . . which it was not even allowed to exploit fully.

These few case histories are extremely important for various reasons. For one, they show that what Westerners regard as successes are not necessarily seen in the same light by the Japanese. Far more significant, they show that what Westerners regard as the keys to success may not open many doors in Japan while other keys, ones they hardly think of, are crucial.

What it takes to win is not, as most foreigners assume, exceptional technological ability, superior quality, a caring personnel system, or even a sense of mission. It is much more banal. Winners must have plenty of financial backing—indispensable to expanding production rapidly and getting through the periods of overcapacity and plummeting profits. They must have an extensive, preferably captive, distribution network as it is the main access to consumers. And they should partially control those they do business with through shareholding, placing of personnel, advancing of loans, or whatever. Then, even with just ordinary quality, ordinary price, and an ability to copy the competitors, they can still rise to the top.

In *The Art of Japanese Management*, Pascale and Athos presented their view of what makes Japanese companies successful, namely the Seven S's. They were: superordinate goals, strategy, structure, systems, skills, style, and staff.[26] Not only were most of these inapplicable, they do not really differentiate winners from losers in Japan. Every company is reasonably proficient and none stands out particularly. Thus, I still prefer my own Seven C's, introduced in *Japan As—Anything But—Number One* partly in jest, but surely more accurate.

The Seven C's are: cash, collateral, control, collusion, connivance, copying, and concern. Cash means a very strong financial position, strong enough to outlast rivals during serious bouts of competition. Collateral refers to the distribution network, a means of keeping your distributors loyal. Control should be exercised on your subcontractors so that they do your bidding. Collusion alternates with competition, when rivals keep prices high to recover from earlier losses. Connivance is with the government, necessary to obtain authorizations or financial support. Copying. That should be obvious by now. Concern? It is useful to inform the consumers just how much you seek their satisfaction and the workers just how much you appreciate their support . . . whether you mean it or not. ∎

Notes

1. Pascale and Athos, *The Art of Japanese Management*.

2. Abegglen and Stalk, *Kaisha*, pp. 46-52.

3. Kuniyasu Sakai, "The Feudal World of Japanese Manufacturing," *Harvard Business Review*, November-December 1990, p. 45.

4. *Far Eastern Economic Review*, August 10, 1989, p. 50.

5. *Wall Street Journal*, August 8, 1989.

6. Vogel, *Japan As Number One*, p. 194.

7. *Wall Street Journal*, April 11, 1991.

8. This was echoed at Honda. "We'd become so big, we'd gotten flabby," was the comment of CEO Kawamoto. "Key decisions couldn't be made until we had gathered a large number of people." *Business Tokyo*, June 1991, p. 21.

9. Arai, *An Intersection of East and West*, p. 150.

10. *Japan Economic Journal*, June 8, 1991.

11. See Woronoff, *The No-Nonsense Guide To Doing Business in Japan* for further advice on how to deal with Japanese employees and companies.

12. On targeting practices including case histories of the declining sectors, see Woronoff, *Japanese Targeting.*

13. *Japan Economic Journal*, July 27, 1991.

14. *The Economist*, August 19, 1989, p. 51.

15. *Financial Times*, November 27, 1990.

16. "Corporate Money Machines," *Far Eastern Economic Review*, July 28, 1988, pp. 78-79.

17. On the Lockheed, Recruit, and many other business scandals, see Woronoff, *Politics, The Japanese Way.*

18. On malpractices in the securities business, see Albert J. Alletzhauser, *The House of Nomura.*

19. *The Economist*, August 3, 1991, p. 16.

20. See Eiji Toyoda, *Toyota, Fifty Years in Motion*, and Toyota Motor Corp., *Toyota, A History of the First 50 Years.*

21. *The Economist*, January 17, 1987, p. 74.

22. Abegglen and Stalk, op. cit., pp. 46-52.

23. For the Sony story, see Morita, *Made in Japan.*

24. For the Matsushita story, albeit through rose-colored glasses, see Pascale and Athos, op. cit.

25. Ibid., p. 30.

26. Ibid., pp. 80-84.

7

Learning from Japan

Beware the Overzealous Teacher!

■ One of the more remarkable intellectual fashions to catch on not only in the West, or nearby Asia, but virtually around the globe, has been the idea of "learning from Japan." This turned out to be anything but a passing fancy. It has been in vogue for decades already. The number of areas in which one is urged to learn is amazingly extensive, from education to martial arts. But the most intensive effort has surely been to teach the world Japanese-style management.

Japanese management, as an object of emulation, covers a rather broad range of sub-sectors. It involves the management of things, such as plant design and use of robotics, but its primary focus is people, be they blue-collar or white-collar workers. For the former, there is quality control, productivity, and a degree of "caring." For the latter, there are the secrets of harmonious cooperation and involvement, whether through bottom-up decision-making or group-based teamwork. Increasingly, there is also interest in corporate planning and strategy for top executives.

However, regardless of what the pundits preach, it would not be wise to rush into embracing all things Japanese. For one, as has been amply shown already, many aspects of Japanese management are not as good as claimed. Even the better features sometimes have negative aspects or hidden weaknesses. And then there are some techniques which are simply inefficient or foolish. It would be extremely dangerous to borrow those from Japan. Foreign companies have enough troubles without adding to them!

This concern is most pertinent at a time when Japanese management is being questioned and criticized at home and is undergoing far-reaching changes and reforms. It would not hurt to heed Kunio Odaka's warning to potential sorcerer apprentices:

> ... the myth claims that Japanese management will work well in other countries just as it has worked well in Japan. Although foreign businessmen are certainly free to try to learn all they can from Japanese management, the disadvantages of Japanese management are coming to outweigh the advantages even in Japan. How can a system which is not even performing as expected at home hope to perform as expected elsewhere?[1]

Yet another problem is that many aspects of Japanese management are rooted in Japanese culture. Things are done in a given way because of traditions or social mores. Admittedly, many of the techniques were really concocted by management and imposed on labor, but that was facilitated by certain predispositions. It would thus be much harder to apply them elsewhere and, even if they were accepted, the results might be quite different. That's another reason not to adopt them without second thoughts.[2]

None of this is said with the intent that we should dismiss the idea of learning from Japan. It is essential for every society to be open to new concepts and emulate the best that comes from outside. In the case of Japan, since it has been an economic success, there is yet more reason to seek out positive lessons. Still, this must be done carefully and intelligently. It is indispensable to take only what is truly useful and reject the rest. And there is little point to adopting features that are not transportable and will not grow in other cultural environments.

This is frequently ignored by authors who propone the adoption of Japanese ways insistently and indiscriminately. Too many of them just claim that, if it worked for Japan, it must work for us. But they do not do their homework and verify that a given technique or practice actually worked for Japan. Nor do they check how such techniques and practices fared abroad. Fortunately, other writers have looked into these questions and their conclusions will be considered. In so doing, practice must be given precedence over theory and actual experiences can help better understand the problems.

This chapter will look at the situation from various angles. First, it is worthwhile to review the management reforms ongoing in Japan, to see which aspects the Japanese themselves are modifying or discarding. Further insight can be gained by noting which management techniques the Japanese are applying in their own overseas operations. After all, "we would not expect non-Japanese firms to transplant successfully if the Japanese do not do so themselves."[3] This done, it is much easier to select some useful lessons to learn and discern those practices which are both positive and transferable.

Reforming Japanese Management

While foreign management gurus and friendly academics admired and praised Japanese management from afar, those who actually had to live with it often found the system wanting. There has been constant criticism from all levels. Top executives, especially the more entrepreneurial, complained about the lacks and limitations. Middle-managers grumbled about their crushing burden. Ordinary workers griped about the daily toil and the more ambitious were annoyed at being held back. This was echoed by the media which has attacked one aspect after another.

Grumblings did not remain just idle talk. By the 1960s, and then more energetically with the oil shocks of the 1970s and the *endaka* crisis of the 1980s, Japanese authorities tried to do something about it. Plans and recommendations issued forth from business organizations and trade unions alike. The task was taken up by the Japan Productivity Council, which realized that after having rationalized factories it was time to do something about the offices. Meanwhile, here and there, specific companies adopted specific measures to correct specific abuses. When they succeeded, the idea spread and clear tendencies emerged. While the ultimate destination remains uncertain, there is no doubt that the reform movement is advancing.

Although there were many individual grievances, they can be summed up under several headings (many of which are already familiar from reading this book). Among other things, there was an excessive institutionalization and bureaucratization of management which left companies relatively sclerotic. It was harder than ever to reach decisions, let alone implement them. More and more managers rising to positions of authority could follow, but not formulate, orders. There was a distressing lack of vigor, to say nothing of imagination or creativity. And there was too little rationality to counteract habit and precedent.

This was exacerbated by growing concerns over rising personnel costs. Companies were no longer expanding as rapidly and financial resources were harder to come by. Yet, they were saddled with large numbers of employees who had been hired in better times and had to be carried another 10, 20, or 30 years. They had all been promised a managerial post ultimately, but there was not enough for so many managers to do and they were too expensive. This problem at the top was compounded by one at the bottom. New recruits were quite different. They wanted to get ahead faster, based more on ability than seniority. And they wanted less hassle.

These assorted goals and pressures generated various reforms, the single most important being a shift from promotion by seniority to one by performance. This "merit" promotion system, which was introduced very widely, was most promising. It should make it possible to allow more competent or dynamic employees to advance more rapidly, while also rewarding them for past effort and providing an incentive for all to work harder. It would also encourage employees to show more initiative and creativity in order to stand out from the rest.

Unfortunately, much of this was at variance with the traditional values. Workers had been taught in the company, in school, and at home, not to stand out or show initiative. While some, especially the more talented and younger ones, wanted to benefit, older ones feared this was just a trick to do them out of promotions and wage hikes. Thus, many workers were against the reform and the personnel managers expected to implement it were worried about dissafection. In addition, how could they evaluate merit? There were no objective criteria, employees did not even have job descriptions, and when tasks were accomplished by groups it was hard to tell who did what.

The result was that, rather than judge employees, they were asked to judge themselves. There were annual evaluation interviews in which potential managers would rate themselves.

They were thus faced with a dilemma. If they praised themselves too highly, they would be regarded as boastful, a vice in Japan. If they were too modest, they might not get that promotion.[4] Still, the self-evaluation combined with evaluation by personnel managers and superiors did play a growing role. While hardly meeting the original expectations, "merit" was increasingly taken into account for wage hikes and promotions, accounting for 30 percent of the total promotions in many companies but 50 percent or more in dynamic ones like Sony or Honda.[5]

Another way of weeding out both underachievers and those without much initiative proved much simpler. New employees were just asked whether they wanted to be on a career track eventually leading to the top or whether they were satisfied with an ordinary job. They would then not be forced to relocate at the company's whim or carry the burden of management. As noted earlier, the two-track system was partly designed to sidetrack women. But there were ever more men who felt the sacrifices were too great and happily accepted a softer alternative, even if it meant lower wages and less promotion.

Yet, there were still too many men hired under the initial "lifetime" grant, men who had reached their forties and fifties and expected a managerial post. To satisfy them, at first, companies just created jobs, many of which had no special responsibilities or even any subordinates. And the older men were happy with the title. Soon, however, there were too many layers of management and it was realized that, like it or not, some had to go. This could be done by early retirement (with a larger pension) or transfer to a subsidiary or supplier (considerably less gentle). But Toyota and Honda went much further, abolishing whole management categories.

To increase know-how and competence, there was grudging acceptance of the need for specialization. This was to be enhanced in two ways. One was to recruit more mid-career or entry-level personnel on the basis of experience or training in the desired subject. The other was to create more specialist posts and sometimes whole specialist career tracks. Still, to make this popular, it was necessary to enhance the status and rewards of specialists over generalists, something that was obviously obstructed by the latter. Here, too, the reform was partly aborted although specialists have become increasingly visible, not only in high tech companies, but also retailers like Seibu.[6]

Improving creativity was obviously a more difficult endeavor. You can go around proselytizing and haranguing. You can lecture employees on the need to think independently. But, when this goes against everything they have been taught and the rewards are few (especially in a society where standing out is more likely to be penalized), the results will remain meager. Thus, the creativity drives accomplished much less than the earlier productivity drives. Still, there were signs of change, and at least now top management was leaning in the right direction. For example, in 1988, Nissan adopted a new policy of "promotion of diversity, respect for specialization and individuality," which encouraged this concretely.[7]

It is clear that Japan's managers were exerting great efforts and showing some ingenuity in reforming the white-collar side. This effort, it must be mentioned, was obviously the less efficient. When it came to the factories, the blue-collar workers were energized more directly. They were simply ordered to work harder and come up with more suggestions. Meanwhile, to be sure productivity rose, jobs were further rationalized and more workers were replaced by machinery or robots. In expanding industries, redundant workers were moved into other jobs; in declining ones, they were fired or transferred out one way or the other.

But there was little sense in reforming the way ordinary employees worked if nothing were done at the top. It was unmistakably clear that it was no longer possible to expand indefinitely and some other goal had to be found. One was diversification. But that served little purpose if everybody diversified into the same sector, following the leaders. Upgrading products when everybody came out with new models so quickly that the product cycle was shortened proved equally fruitless. Under these circumstances, competitive battles would be far more punishing and winners would be fewer.

Thus, in the 1980s, managers thought ever less of expansion, diversification, and scale economies and ever more of—guess what?—profit. Of course, they were not yet willing to sacrifice market share. Especially not if they feared that their rivals had not forsaken it and might squeeze them out. Still, it was evident that profitability was rising in esteem. This was shown by the 1987 U.S.-Japan Comparative Survey of Corporate Behavior. The Japanese rated profits almost as highly as U.S. companies, downgrading turnover and market share.[8] This trend has been confirmed by corporate policy, one of the most significant signs being Toyota's recent decision to do away with numeric market share targets.

While the progress has been limited, and some reforms were stymied or distorted, it is clear that there is more to come. Just which changes are most likely can be sensed from a survey of personnel officers by Sanno College. They were asked which trends they expected to shape the system by the year 2000. Some of the biggest changes would be a dramatic increase in mid-career employment (90 percent) with ever less workers staying in one company throughout a "lifetime" stint (70 percent). Meanwhile, employees would increasingly choose jobs rather than companies (70 percent) while the wage and severance pay rate structures changed radically (60 percent). But they did not expect the situation to vary much in other respects, namely that recruiting on the basis of ability and skill would make seniority meaningless or that wages would be based largely on performance. And no one expected much improvement in the status of women.[9]

From what has been done so far and what can be expected in the future, it must be obvious that these reforms will gradually align the Japanese system on Western, if not necessarily U.S., practices. So, there is a degree of convergence. Western academics or managers who too eagerly embrace the system may find that they have adopted aspects the Japanese already shed or are trying to get rid of.

Finally, although there is some convergence, this does not spell the demise of the Japanese system. Rather, since most of the reforms are only partial, it is just a revamping and reshaping. What is happening is much easier to grasp in connection with the idea of a "core" system. There will still be a hard core of employees, namely those males on the career track, who will enter the company on graduation and stay with it until retirement. They will, however, be a smaller core surrounded by more second-track employees, mid-career hires, specialists, women, and temporary workers. Within the core, there will be more emphasis on merit and rationality, but loyalty and seniority will still play a role. After all, this smaller core must hold together if it is to dominate a larger peripheral workforce.

Japanese Managing Foreigners

It would seem that, if anyone were eager to introduce Japanese methods abroad, it would be the Japanese firms which have set up offshore subsidiaries. They are trying to run manufacturing or service establishments as efficiently as possible and usually assume that their own methods are best. Naturally, they would want to replace inferior local techniques. In any event, Japanese methods are the only ones many of the managers are familiar with or use effectively.

This urge is only tempered by an intellectual realization that these are, indeed, foreign countries and foreign workers who have different customs and practices. But much of the talk of "when in Rome" and adapting to local conditions is just lip service. Still, when the Japanese forget this need, which happens often enough, they are rudely reminded by local workers and politicians who react negatively and angrily. The Japanese, then, are aware that they must adjust their methods.

The result has been a rather limited and mitigated transference of Japanese management.[10] The extent varies partly with the country. In countries whose culture is closer to theirs, namely parts of East and Southeast Asia, there is a larger degree of change. In backward countries whose own industrial traditions are weak, there is even more, since Japan is filling a relative void. In older industrial nations, there is a tendency to merely overlay some Japanese aspects on the existing system. There, the Japanese share can be quite meager. In no country, even those most similar culturally like Korea or Taiwan, have they imported the system in its entirety.[11]

The situation also differs from factories to offices. In the factories, not surprisingly, the Japanese install excellent machinery and equipment, although not always the very best. For instance, in developing countries, labor is cheaper so little is gained by greater automation. Also, especially in advanced nations, they would not want their rivals to learn their very latest production secrets. Still, compared to local companies or other expatriates, the Japanese have some of the most efficient and productive operations.[12]

They also get along reasonably well with the blue-collar staff. Since ordinary workers have a lower status in developing and advanced societies alike, the mere gestures of everybody eating in the same canteen, using the same parking lot, or being called "associate" is appreciated. Japanese managers also try to get to know the workers, find out their desires and grievances, and even satisfy them when possible. But this "equality" is rather superficial, since Japanese companies have fought unionization more bitterly than most and thereby deny workers any true equality in power terms.

It has been noted that the workers frequently back management in this dislike of unions and not surprisingly. The Japanese recruit more carefully than any other nationality, screening out former union members, even former workers, and inducting those who seem to dislike unionization or are more pliant. To the extent possible, they also locate operations in non-union areas, showing a particular predilection for those with a traditional work ethic. In so doing, at least in the U.S., they avoid hiring Blacks and Hispanics.[13]

Blue-collar workers are organized somewhat along Japanese lines. They are given looser job descriptions which permit them to handle more different tasks as needed. They are formed into groups as much as possible, applying a teamwork approach that many appreciate. There are sporadic attempts to turn them into company men and women, although if there is resistance, the managers often back off. Still, in many factories, workers wear the company uniform, cap and badge, and even sing the company song. There is certainly an effort to have workers engage in quality control or make suggestions, but this is far less compulsive than in Japan and participation is rewarded in more palpable manners.

Japanese factories also engage in a certain amount of just-in-time delivery, although this is limited by the weakness of local suppliers. Rather than strengthen them, the trend has been to invite Japanese suppliers to set up shop locally to service the same patron as back home. This makes it much easier to expand the Japanese system. In general, there is a marked tendency for Japanese firms to deal with one another more than local firms, not only for suppliers, but banks, transport, and construction companies.

When running offices, the situation is quite different. The Japanese try considerably less to impose their standard practices than adapt to Western ones. They hire specialists rather than generalists, they lay down job classifications, and clarify lines of responsibility. Alas, not having much experience with this, the

Japanese are apparently rather poor at specifying who does what and tend to expect everybody to pitch in when there is work to be done. Thus, there is still more fuzziness between jobs and uncertainty as to who is responsible for what than in Western firms.

Unlike the factory workers, white-collar employees who have undergone special training and have specific skills do not enjoy this ambiguity. They do not like having others intervene in their sphere or being expected to help out with something that does not regard them. In addition, they want to be evaluated for what they do best and not some general devotion to duty. Their concern only increases if they feel that they are not being evaluated on how well they perform as opposed to how much they help the company. As it happens, this is not only a grievance of Western employees but Asians as well.[14]

Any general malaise becomes more specific in connection with promotions. Most foreign personnel, both Western and other Asian, expect to be promoted on the basis of how they perform individually and not on how they participate in the group. Those who do better expect to be rewarded more. They do not want to move slowly in lock-step. Yet, even when they agree in principle, Japanese managers find it hard to evaluate staff on performance or single out some for special reward. They are not trying to impose a career escalator or incipient seniority system, but it sometimes seems that way. So the potential high-flyers and stars get very frustrated while waiting.

To defuse such potential friction, as in the factory, Japanese managers try to "get to know the locals" better, even to the extent of drinking with them in the evening. There is an attempt at bottom-up decision-making, with all levels consulted before important decisions. But this is more complicated when many of the subordinates are foreign while the superiors are largely Japanese. The mood can become particularly ugly if the managers speak Japanese among themselves, which the rest do not understand, or hold other meetings or after-hours chats to finalize decisions.

As noted, there is already some frustration over promotions. This is accentuated by the widespread feeling that locals can go only so far and that top positions will always be held by Japanese. This is further exacerbated by the fact that the Japanese tend to impose more of their own kind than do, say, Americans in Japan or other foreigners abroad. They are especially slow in recruiting locals to top positions. Even then, many foreign managers sense that they are not truly in charge. There is a "shadow" executive out there, some Japanese in the head office or, worse, one of their own subordinates, who is really calling the shots.[15]

This brings us to "lifetime" employment. The Japanese rarely promise this and, even in Japan, it is a tacit agreement. But they do hint that they will reward loyalty more than others and job security is somewhat greater. In some instances, when business was slow, companies even had workers paint the factory or tend the lawns rather than fire them. But that was probably because they expected to expand later and needed the workers. Once the expansion phase is over, the Japanese will probably lay off workers like anyone else. This was already shown in some developing countries when companies were just closed down, among the Japanese brokers in New York when trading slackened, and most visibly when Bridgestone dropped 3,000 ex-Firestone workers.

But hire-and-fire practices are standard in most societies and these employees would find it difficult to believe that the Japanese are different. More serious consequences can arise for the Japanese through selective resignations. They often lose their best employees, those who show more initiative or feel they cannot go any further. Those who stay on are often the less competent, less ambitious, less valuable. The Japanese could well end up with a bunch of "B" level people, as one keen observer put it.[16]

Another category of employees used poorly, and frequently disgruntled, is women in general. This occurs less on the assembly line, where they have simple jobs and limited aspirations. But those who are specialized or seek managerial positions are routinely relegated to lower-level jobs, with less chance of promotion, and have trouble dealing with Japanese managers, all of them men, who are unaccustomed to treating women as equals. Most of this dissatisfaction merely resulted in women quitting sooner than otherwise or preemptively avoiding employment in Japanese firms. But there have been lawsuits for sexual bias.

Finally, there is the question of profitability. Most other countries operate on the basis of profit and not market share, a basic urge the Japanese must temper. There is no doubt that, if left alone, they would push constantly and aggressively for market share even if it drives out the local competition. As guests, however, they find this conduct less becoming. And they are afraid that the local government will react, as it frequently does, by imposing restrictions or restraints. Gradually, as they are acclimated, and become part of the foreign business culture, Japanese businessmen also realize the charms of greater profitability. This is understood equally well back in Tokyo, where top executives have to justify the costs of investments.

Yet, although Japanese companies abroad are clearly shooting more for profitability, they rarely attain it. MITI statistics have shown repeatedly that the return on investment of Japanese overseas subsidiaries is very poor.[17] That might have been expected in early years, when the ventures were still young. After all, the Japanese seek long-term gains. But even ventures that are 20 and 30 years old are not performing well and don't even keep up with local enterprises which are less efficient.[18]

There are various and sundry reasons for this. Since the Japanese want the very best in productive machinery, they spend more on factories and equipment than they might. When they acquire local establishments, they often pay far too much. Worse, the Japanese pay in yen which has tended to appreciate against most other currencies. Thus, any dollars earned are worth less when converted, with baht or cruzeiros faring even less well. But that cannot be all. It is hard to escape the feeling that, never having cared overly about profits back home, Japanese managers abroad simply do not know how to achieve a good bottom line.

Lessons and Non-Lessons

In seeking instructive lessons, as must be obvious by now, Japan is more likely to provide a good model in the factory than in the office, for blue-collar workers than white-collar employees, for lower level staff than top executives. It is also more worthy of emulation with regard to management of things than people, unless those people happen to be Japanese. If they are anything else, whether Western or Oriental, from advanced or developing countries, one should proceed very carefully. That, by the way, is what the Japanese have done abroad themselves.

But using the Japanese as models does not necessarily mean that you should copy them, that you should do everything the way they do. Sometimes their way is not the best way to achieve the same goal. Sometimes the Japanese themselves are not happy with it. Whatever the lesson, adapt and adjust. Moreover, never go all the way. The Japanese always make their worst mistakes when they push a good idea too far or use a good technique too much or, in some other manner, overdo and exaggerate. Each lesson should be applied with moderation, periodically testing that you have not reached the point of diminishing returns or, worse, the point where more means less.

In fact, for many of the lessons, the basic thrust may not even be that Westerners or others should stop what they are doing and do like the Japanese. Rather, they should simply realize that they are going too far with their own practices which no longer produce the desired results. They can perhaps correct their excesses by moving in the Japanese direction part way. For example, the corrective to hire-and-fire is not lifetime employment, it is just more job security. The corrective to overspecialization is not Japanese-style generalists but somewhat more job enlargement.

As suggested, the best place to start applying Japanese techniques is in the factory. That is where the Japanese have really done an excellent job. And, as noted, improvements there can raise productivity most. Plenty can be gained from improved plant layout. The handier the equipment, the better a person relates to the task, the more efficient production becomes. Naturally, the introduction of more and better machinery will help, whether this be conventional automation or greater use of robots. They can be combined for flexible production as well. If you are looking for ideas, send your engineers off to visit Japanese factories.

Lean manufacturing makes perfectly good sense even if it is less urgent in countries with more space, or cheaper space, in which to store parts and sub-units. Just-in-time techniques are rather neutral culturally and could be widely adopted. It is certainly useful to integrate suppliers more closely in the production process so that they know what should be prepared and when it should be delivered as much in advance as possible. In so doing, longer leads generate less pressure, so it would be unwise to follow the Japanese in their exaggerated shortening of lead time and delivery deadlines.

This cooperation and integration, however, involves people as well as things and, in particular, affects existing relations between assemblers and suppliers. The latter will be expected to improve quality, lower price, and deliver more rapidly, for all of which they expect some benefit. Since, in most other countries, suppliers are either more independent or at least independent-minded, they may not like the additional constraints and loss of autonomy. So the transition will have to be slower, gentler, and perhaps less far-reaching, while giving them advantages as well.

A lot can also be learned in dealing with blue-collar workers.[19] The simplest thing, often with little or no cost, is merely for supervisors and managers to treat ordinary workers with a bit more courtesy and respect. By now, they have had enough of management's petty perks and simple gestures such as everybody using the same canteen, no special reserved parking for higher-ups, or more frequent visits to the shop floor, would not hurt. Where there are residual class and other distinctions, they could at least be softened. As noted, in Japan, much of this is quite superficial and there is no reason to believe it would be more sincere anywhere else.

Enhancing productivity through participation of the workforce is crucial. This can be done partly with quality control circles, suggestion boxes, and other techniques, and it can be incorporated in an endless process of *kaizen*. But it must involve genuine participation if it is to succeed, at least in the West. Workers should do this on company time, with some sort of remuneration for the time spent, and any rewards for particularly good projects or suggestions should be more material than moral. The effort should also be voluntary and less compulsive than in Japan, otherwise workers will come to hate it and, being less inhibited or controlled, sabotage the campaign.

When it comes to the offices and white-collar employees, it is much harder to find aspects of Japanese management that either contribute to efficiency or harmony or could be readily assimilated in the West and sometimes even in Asia. But there are some. Perhaps the most important is to seek greater stability in the ranks. Abruptly firing employees is not only a misfortune for them, it harms the company. It entails a waste of experience and training and a lack of qualified workers when business turns up again. The mere fear of layoffs can undermine the work will and encourage employees to get out early. There is already enough job-hopping without inciting more.

Stability would be further enhanced by a promotion policy that recognizes more than just ability or performance. Of course, these factors are extremely important in running a dynamic and innovative company. They should be rewarded. But there is no reason they should be rewarded as much. After all, other characteristics are also valuable, in particular loyalty to the company. Loyalty involves not only a willingness to stick with it in hard times, it makes for more experienced workers who are more willing to make sacrifices. If, in Japan, the merit rating can be increased, then surely the loyalty rating can be increased elsewhere.

Part and parcel of this should be greater promotion from within the company rather than turning to outsiders. A constant stream of newcomers, unfamiliar with the company (whatever their other qualifications), is unsettling and disruptive. It is especially so if the purpose, or hidden agenda, of these newcomers is to shake up and reshape the company in their own image of what it should be. Companies can take only so much restructuring without losing their bearings.

If the newcomers parachute into top positions, and then set about hiring their buddies, this will block the promotional chances of those who have been with the company longer and have a legitimate hope of rising. When this hope is cut off, obviously they will perform less well and also think of leaving. The worst situation is when the ranks of personnel which entered at lower levels and gained experience in the company are replaced by a batch of MBAs whose own experience is based on book learning and often short stints in assorted other companies.

This is not a call for lifetime employment. That would be ridiculous. Even in Japan it does not work fully and in other countries, where employees are more individualistic and ambitious, you simply could not hold on to enough staff throughout a career. But the introduction of some of the above features would at least increase the average length of stay. And this would give the company a stability and consistency it often lacks.

What about profitability? Is it a goal too sacred to be touched? Maybe once, but not any more. It is painfully obvious that conventional methods of achieving a good bottom line can no longer overlook the question of market share. Even the fattest profits will be short-lived if market share keeps falling. It is thus necessary to balance both. Market share is particularly important when competing with the Japanese in your own market or, more decisively, in theirs. Once again, this should not be taken to Japan's extremes and even when pressing for market share it is essential to strive for the best return that can be achieved under these circumstances.

Alongside the positive features, which should be adopted and can usually be assimilated, there are some aspects which should be rejected out of hand. It does not make much sense to have companies run by pure generalists who are so busy moving from job to job that they never acquire any technical skills, let alone a specialization. Personnel should still be hired on the basis of what they know, given specific tasks that are clearly laid down (although perhaps less narrowly defined than at present), and on which they will be evaluated. The Japanese admit this. Nor should they get into the company to begin with just because they graduated from Harvard or Oxford or whatever is regarded as a "good" school. They should be judged on their own merits.

Some practices should be avoided. It is ludicrous, as well as discriminatory, to treat women and minorities as poorly as the Japanese do. It is much wiser to adopt policies which will get the best out of every category of worker rather than create some which are kept down so that others may rise more easily. Nor is there much sense in tangling with organized labor or trying to create docile workers who are overly dependent on the company. This could actually be counterproductive.

With regard to certain other "lessons" that appeal to one management *guru* or another, they are not so much dangerous as silly or futile. Mainstream Japanese managers of mainstream Japanese companies do not apply *zen*, or martial arts, or other exotic techniques to enlighten or activate their workers or overcome competitors. Those who do are usually in the outer fringes and generally regarded as such. So appeals for *zen*, vagueness, and the like or reading *The Book of Five Rings* will not get foreign managers very far.[20] If anything, they would be more confused than ever.

It is equally misleading to assume that Japanese managers are particularly high-minded. Yes, they do make very noble statements on occasion.[21] They have very uplifting and moralistic company slogans about helping the people, serving the customer, or relentlessly pursuing quality. It's an old habit. Japanese companies once adopted similar mottos about serving the nation and worshipping the emperor. Anyway, these sentiments do not have much to do with practice. For example, "contribute to society" was the primary mission of Recruit Company, involved in a major insider trading and influence buying scandal. "Prosper along with the client," and "maintain a nationwide perspective" were missions of Nomura Securities, caught in an even bigger scandal. That may have been because "strive to stay ahead" took precedence.

Still, if management "experts" and their clients think that refurbishing their slogans and refining their philosophies will help, let them proceed. At least, it may have a positive PR impact. But it won't help them compete against the Japanese, whose sentiments will be even nobler, yet will not keep them from making that last sale when push comes to shove.[22] Anyone who foolishly thinks that it will has obviously missed an essential point.

The Japanese play hard ball. If you play soft ball, you are bound to lose.

Finally, the heavy emphasis placed on Japan's care for the workers, love of harmony, urge to make the best use of people and the like betrays considerable ignorance of Japanese realities.[23] As amply shown, none of this applies much to small companies, companies in backward sectors, subcontractors, temporary workers, or women. Nor does it even have much relevance to those who enjoy "lifetime" employment. Japanese management runs as smoothly as it does because of manipulation and subtle exploitation. If you ever forget that and just try to be "nice" to people, you will never make any of the Japanese lessons stick. ■

Notes

1. Odaka, op. cit., p. 4.

2. Here one can agree with Toyohiro Kono that it is best to distinguish between culture-related and relatively culture-free practices and adopt only the former. "Generally speaking, most aspects of the Japanese personnel management system took shape after the war as a result of rational thinking rather than the unique culture of Japan, so to a great extent they are transferable to other countries. . . . Any system that originates in the core of the culture, however, is not transferable." Toyohiro Kono, *Strategy & Structure of Japanese Enterprises*, p. 176.

3. Solomon B. Levine and Makoto Ohtsu, "Transplanting Japanese Labor Relations," in Levine and Taira, *Japan's External Economic Relations*, p. 103.

4. "Salaries Pegged to Merit Review Taking Hold," *Japan Economic Journal*, March 30, 1991, p. 34.

5. It must not have appealed to Deming that his favorite pupils should do such a thing, to judge by his solemn warning: "Is Japanese management to become infected with the disease of Western management? Rating people? Is Japanese management going to become infected?" Apparently so. Walton, *The Deming Management Method*, p. 248.

6. *Tokyo Business Today*, April 1990, p. 38.

7. Ibid., p. 37.

8. *Tokyo Business Today*, November 1988, p. 42.

9. *Yomiuri*, December 13, 1990.

10. This has been confirmed in a comprehensive survey of the relevant literature by Levine and Ohtsu, op. cit., p. 116. "The systematic evidence available shows that only in a few cases has there been any wholesale transplanting of Japanese labor relations even with the rapid step-up of foreign direct investment from Japan. Far more cases report either adaptation to host country practices or, at most, selective transfer of practices that are not necessarily Japanese alone."

11. For more on the transfer of Japanese practices, see David W. Edgington, *Japanese Business Down Under*, K. John Fukuda, *Japanese-Style Management Transferred*, Kazuo Shibagaki et al, *Japanese and European Management, Their International Adaptability*, and Shoichi Yamashita, *Transfer of Japanese Technology and Management to the Asean Countries*.

12. See Woronoff, *Japan's Commercial Empire*.

13. Interesting case studies of Japanese operations in America are Joseph and Suzy Fucini, *Working for the Japanese*, and David Gelsanliter, *Jump Start: Japan Comes to the Heartland*.

14. See Yamashita, op. cit.

15. See Vladimir Pucik, Mitsuyo Harada, and George Fifield, *Management Culture and the Effectiveness of Local Executives in Japanese-Owned U.S. Corporations*, Ann Arbor, University of Michigan, 1989.

16. James A. Cramer, "Japanese Management Deficient Abroad," *Japan Economic Journal*, July 6, 1991.

17. Ministry of International Trade and Industry, *Overseas Activities of Japanese Business Enterprises*, annual.

18. Woronoff, op. cit., pp. 362-369.

19. For useful comments on which techniques can be borrowed, see Cole, *Work, Mobility & Participation*, pp. 251-263.

20. For a taste of this, see Pascale and Athos, "Zen and the Art of Management," in *The Art of Japanese Management*, pp. 85-115.

21. This tendency can be clearly observed in the writings of Japanese business leaders, with Konosuke Matsushita going somewhat further than most. See Matushita, *Not For Bread Alone* and *Quest for Prosperity*.

22. Bill Ouchi, on the other hand, seems to believe in the efficacy of noble thoughts to judge by the space devoted to company philosophies in *Theory Z*.

23. This line has apparently been swallowed by many U.S. and some European "experts," including Pascale and Athos, Ouchi, Vogel, Dore, and others too numerous too mention. Japanese managers, workers, academics, and the general public are much more skeptical.

8

Their Weaknesses, Your Strengths

Western Spirit, Japanese Learning

■ More than a century ago, when Japan was forcibly opened to the West, the Japanese were painfully aware of their inferiority in certain crucial endeavors, especially science and defense. They also realized that Westerners were well ahead of them economically. Unlike many other peoples in a similar situation, they did not reject the foreigners' superiority or make believe it did not exist, but rather set about most purposefully to adopt any possible strong points. In so doing, however, they were not willing to surrender what they regarded as higher values. The formula they struck upon was *Wakon yosai* or "Japanese spirit, Western learning."

As it happens, at the present time many foreigners, including Westerners, Asians, and others, have finally come to recognize Japan's superiority in some significant sectors. Most of the strongest developments are related to technology and economics. Thus, these students of Japan decided to learn more from the Japanese in order to better resist or beat them. But they are no more willing to give up their own culture and traditions than the Japanese. It might thus seem reasonable for them to adopt the slogan "Western spirit, Japanese learning," in which the word Western could be freely replaced by American, British, Malaysian, and so on.

Exactly how they can achieve this goal is uncertain. But part of the solution must surely be to adopt those facets of Japanese management which are helpful. This is in line with the concept of "learning from Japan." There are many things to learn, even after striking those processes that are inefficient or untransferable. So, there is no reason why companies should not make every effort to improve plant layout, install better machinery, produce to a larger scale, and expand, if necessary, by exporting. None of this has much to do with spirit and can be readily accomplished.

Even where spirit must be considered, appreciable progress can be made by improving relations between ordinary workers and supervisors and having workers participate more in quality control and productivity enhancement. With suitably adapted techniques in their best interest, employees would doubtlessly cooperate. Techniques that temper individualism and egoism of employees and replace it with greater harmony and loyalty can be applied in the offices. Even chief executives would gain by having a longer-term view of things.

All this should be done, and done diligently, and done until the lessons are thoroughly learned. But it is still necessary to accomplish this while the Japanese are attacking your market effectively and you are still trying to get into theirs and finding it hard to crack. In short, the situation is dynamic, not static. Thus, it is essential to consider how both sides interact.

By knowing more about how the Japanese enter markets and expand, it may be easier to hold them off. It may also help when you decide to tackle the Japanese market. In these two contests, where Japanese and foreign firms are pitted directly against one another, it is more vital than ever to make full use of your strengths and take even fuller advantage of any weaknesses the competition may show. What can be done is sketched out in three sections, followed by a fourth that outlines some tactics that have been undertaken by specific foreign companies.

Defending the Home Front

Since Japanese companies usually seek market share over profit, they tend to attack foreign markets in ways which differ from other companies or local competitors. They will initially price low, indeed, very low, in order to sell as large quantities as possible. They will push one product or model rather than many. They will also narrow their focus geographically, launching a sales campaign in California or England rather than the U.S. or European community as a whole. They seek to gain a foothold.

Their sales campaigns can be very intensive because they try to pump large quantities of goods into small areas, and will not let up until an acceptable share of that market has been conquered. Then, of course, the foothold will be expanded into broader markets, with more products. From the bottom of the line, the Japanese will gradually work their way toward the top. Thus, the offensive continues relentlessly.

Still, since the attack seems so narrow initially, many local companies fail to realize the significance until it is too late. Time and again, in the U.S., Europe, and Asia this has happened—in textiles, consumer electronics, automobiles, computers, and semiconductors. Among other things, it happened for motorcycles in the U.S. and was not noticed by Harley-Davidson until it was almost too late.

> Honda started out with an inexpensive, lightweight bike that was more a scooter than a motorcycle. It could hardly have been less threatening to Harley, which specialized in big bikes, known as super-heavyweights. Aiming for a new generation of affluent, young, upper-middle-class riders, Honda advertising showed attractive couples on motorcycles and proclaimed, "You Meet the Nicest People on a Honda." Once its beachhead was secured, the Japanese motorcycle maker expanded its product line to go head-to-head with Harley-Davidson in the super-heavyweight class.[1]

Thus, it is best to recognize such an attack and fight back immediately and massively. It is necessary to mobilize whatever resources you possess, tighten your distribution, lower your own prices if need be, and keep the Japanese competitor from getting a foothold. It may seem that the response is exaggerated compared to the present threat, like using a hammer to kill a fly. That may well be so. But whatever the cost, it will be much, much smaller than what could be required later on.

Price is usually critical. When they first try a market, Japanese quality is not necessarily better and, even if it is, local consumers will not yet know. Their products are frequently quite ordinary. After all, they are mass-produced items. So price will be the main selling point. If the price looks too low, not only lower than yours but lower than what the Japanese charge back home, don't hesitate to apply dumping or other laws against unfair trade practices. However, don't assume that this will get you off the hook, proceedings may take too long and decisions come too late.[2] It is best to respond by lowering your own prices as far—or further—even if losses are temporarily incurred.

Meanwhile, keep an eye out for the Japanese company's next step. It could be a new product, in which case you had better produce something comparable. It may be another, nearby market, in which case you should be able to react even quicker. In early stages, the odds are on your side because as a national company you will be more strongly rooted in the market and probably have commensurate technological ability and financial clout.

Things become considerably more serious once the Japanese have caught up technologically and can come out with products you cannot beat. You should thus carefully monitor their R&D activities and any trial launches in Japan so you know what the next product may be. Then you had better match it. Even if this means pulling staff off other research and starting a crash program to develop a me-too product, it must be done. Perhaps you want your company to aspire to more than a reputation of copy-cat, but that is certainly better than ending up as a no-show.

While Japanese companies can be slowed down or contained in earlier phases, eventually they will become significant players. At that point, you should switch tactics. Their distribution ability will probably not be better than yours, but their manufacturing capability may well exceed it, with regard to quality, delivery, price, etc. If they stick to exports, there is not much you can do to reverse the situation. If, on the other hand, they were obliged to take up local production and forced to keep increasing local content, you would be on a more even playing field.

Admittedly, this is not risk or trouble free. The Japanese will still have excellent technologies and first-rate production techniques, they will encourage their workers to pay closer attention to quality, and the workers may be cheaper or more agile if younger or recruited in depressed areas. But the Japanese will be less familiar with the economic environment, unaccustomed to dealing with local workers, occasionally forced to use the same suppliers and, above all, at least initially, operating on smaller scales.

Once again, while transplants can be threatening and Japanese competition will still be nasty, this alternative is usually less formidable than facing exports straight from Japan. Moreover, having settled into the market, the Japanese may be less unruly and disruptive than before.

The following advice is a bit old. But even an old story bears repeating when it has a new wrinkle. Since the Japanese get into the market first on cost, and advanced countries may not be able to produce cheaply enough because of higher labor costs, it is worthwhile having products made in cheaper labor countries, including Southeast Asia and now Mexico. It is the only way to undercut the Japanese. Perhaps you will not make much on the product, but at least you get the margin and protect your base.

What is new is that Japan is no longer as cheap as it used to be. This means it is becoming uncompetitive for a whole range of articles at the lower end of the line. It would be wise for competitors to reclaim them, often by shifting supply to cheaper labor countries. But, in some cases, with relatively cheaper labor due to lower exchange rates and more advanced technology, it may be possible even for the U.S. to get some of these products back. It would be rather silly to regard this also as a less than noble effort. Every additional product adds to the range and manufacturing base and takes away from Japan's base.

This sort of thing can be even more interesting for developing countries, especially those with cheap labor and/or raw materials. They can gradually follow Japan upward, taking over one article after the other. This can be done haphazardly, as opportunities arise, or more systematically, by taking a page from Japan's own targeting techniques. The latter is obviously preferable, for it charts the way ahead and provides a logical progression from simpler to more sophisticated products.[3]

So far, as already explained, the Japanese have done a fairly good job of using blue-collar workers abroad, often better than local companies. But they have repeatedly gotten into difficulty with minorities and women. And they have sometimes made a mess of relationships with white-collar employees, men and women, including those who were the most able and ambitious. Aside from that, according to most observers, they have not been overly successful in processing office work or getting the staff to toil harder or perform better.

This is an opening for local companies. First of all, they should improve morale in the factory, where it is usually lowest, by using some of the techniques the Japanese apply, like quality control, productivity enhancement, job enlargement and improved treatment of the rank-and-file. Then they must gain an edge where the Japanese are weak, most evidently by making better use of women and minorities, and by using more efficient procedures in the office. Unlike the Japanese, who are stuck with B-class employees, they should shoot for A. And they should remain more flexible, not getting bogged down in overly consensual decision-making which even a long-time U.S. manager for Japanese companies rejected.

> With my American managers, I'm somewhat less concerned about reaching 100% consensus agreement. I've learned through experience that collaborative decision-making works virtually as well as the consensual approach. While consensus requires 100% effort to achieve 100% "buy in," collaboration requires

only 20% effort to achieve 80% buy in. I talk or. collaborate with everyone because I've seen the importance of owning a decision; I know people want to be heard and not dictated to. But I have limits about how much time I can afford to take.[4]

Oddly enough, one of the most important measures for fighting back against the Japanese is not only to resist them on the home front but to make an incursion in the Japanese market. The reason the Japanese can do so well abroad is that they have overwhelming control of the domestic market. This permits them to produce goods at huge scales and also sell at pretty much whatever prices makers can agree upon. When they are not engaged in fierce competition, which is actually most of the time, they are milking the Japanese consumer. Earnings are then used to cross-subsidize new products and launch export drives.

Only if foreign companies get in, create some genuine competition, and make it hard for Japanese companies to keep prices high, can they prevent the Japanese from gathering the resources they need to overrun foreign markets. It is worthwhile making such an effort even if the initial costs are high. However, if you pick your products well and market intelligently, you should be generating money rather than using it up. More on that in the next section.

Obviously, selling to Japan has a beneficial effect on foreign companies. They can expand their production base, increase economies of scale, and boost profits. Even more important, they can keep a closer watch on what the Japanese are doing. You cannot afford to wait until the Japanese launch an offensive. You need some advance warning. That can best be provided by whatever office is promoting your Japan operation. In short, if you want to fight the Japanese, you have to do it at both ends.

Competing in Japan

The situation for foreign companies trying to crack the Japanese market is more complex because you have to consider not only how to sell your goods but also, if you set up a local operation, how to manage a company there. For both of these, it is necessary to adapt, to some extent, to Japanese practices and certainly emulate those portions which are superior or more effective. But it would be foolish to go the whole way because, as we have discussed, there are also negative and wasteful aspects.

When launching products in Japan, it is best to do as the Japanese, namely concentrate your fire power. You should pick just one product rather than the entire range you may handle, assuming it is a larger company. That product should be the one with the biggest edge over Japanese counterparts, whether because it is cheaper or offers better quality or both. It may also be a product that is quite unusual, either one that is new to the market or at least has a different design or a cachet of foreignness.[5]

This product should be launched in a limited market, probably a portion of Tokyo or another large city, and not nationwide. This is done not only because you want to concentrate your efforts, but also because it is extremely difficult to find distributors which can market nationwide. And, most will not join in until they know the sales potential is good. Market studies or a small test can help in determining the best location as well as the best product.

You should then give the launch all the backup you can. This includes general advertising, point-of-sale material, and encouraging the individual retailers. You might also send around detail personnel to see how sales are going and offer further support. If the product sells on price, perhaps the price should be cut even more. If it sells on quality or novelty, then more should be invested in personnel, decoration, and service. Whatever the product and strategy, this is a crucial campaign, so make a serious commitment.

The effort and expense will probably be greater than required in most other markets because Japanese consumers are spoiled and take time to be convinced. Equally important, your competitors will be more aggressive in responding than elsewhere. They do not want you to gain a foothold, for that is what you are after. You must get enough market share to justify further measures.

These subsequent measures should be directed toward expansion, whether expansion of market share in depth, by increasing the sales of that first product, or broadening the line, if you have other likely products. It should certainly include an expansion into other geographic regions, more of Tokyo, other large cities and, ultimately, smaller ones. None of this will be easy and each additional step will take another big push.

Timing is extremely significant. While seemingly easier, going in slowly and expanding gradually leaves Japanese competitors time to react. They can increase pressure on existing distributors not to carry your goods and on retailers not to give them good exposure. They can bring down their price or enhance the quality of their own comparable articles. Most important, if you do have something special, they can work on a "me-too" product.

The Japanese are masters at copying. They have spent decades borrowing Western ideas and also copying from one another. Their R&D teams are expert at making minor alterations which result in something different enough not to infringe on proprietary rights, which are not that well-protected in Japan anyway. Worse, they may add some doodads that make their offering more attractive because it is bigger, smaller, cheaper, nicer looking, or whatever.

In fact, you should expect an onslaught of me-too products within a very short time, perhaps a year or so, maybe only a matter of months. And you must be able to react. It would be foolish to wait and see what the competition comes up with before responding. Rather, you should already be preparing to launch a second generation, and thinking about a third, before rivals come out with their first rip-offs. This is the only way to keep ahead.

Eventually, of course, there will be comparable goods on the market and, if you have expanded your foothold, you will be regarded not as a weak foreign interloper or a tame niche producer, but a competitor that must be resisted. If there are now too many players, you can expect periodic bouts of "excessive competition" or *kato kyoso*. This will create the biggest dilemma thus far: do you fight back and how far should you go?

To decide, you must remember that you are in Japan and not back home. The Japanese market is ruled by competition for market share, not profit. You cannot change that and, whether you like it or not, you will find that you have to lower your prices when competitors slash theirs and you will be stuck with slumping profits or mounting losses just like them. Or, the alternative, they will achieve their goal which is, simply put, to drive you out of the market.

To survive in Japan, you must mix the two. You must have some sort of profit to justify the venture. But it is best to lengthen the time horizon for that return and realize that there can be a justifiable trade-off between profit and market share. If need be, you must accept cross-subsidization by other products or financial backing from the head office during serious bouts of competition as a cost of doing business. However, when the Japanese go overboard, it would probably be best not to follow. Accept that you will lose some market share but earn enough to resume more active operations once the bout is over.

Since the Japanese market is so different, it is hard to handle distribution on your own or even find good local distributors. You may need support during competitive bouts, and many foreign companies decide to work with Japanese partners.[6] This makes the choice of the right partner the most important one you are likely to make. Distribution is probably the key, so you must decide which route to follow, whether to stick to exporting, or let a licensee or franchisee handle that aspect. Even in a joint venture, you should pay more attention to the marketing clout than the technological verve of your partner.[7]

However, it is not only a question of finding a partner which can do the most to help you. You want one that actually *will* do its utmost. You must carefully examine both the potential partner and any related firms, particularly those in the group or *keiretsu*, to see whether they are not actual or possible future competitors. You don't want a partner which produces similar goods, or might produce them, or has affiliates that produce them, and would therefore disregard your interests.

If you enter a joint venture, and even more so if you set up your own operation in Japan, you will have to deal with local personnel. Recruiting, training, and effectively using Japanese personnel will be as tough a task as marketing. For one, Japanese personnel is already very expensive. For another, the more promising candidates will not want to work for a foreign firm and it will be necessary to accept what remains. Even those who are competent and hardworking may not be that loyal. Last, and certainly not least, you will find it hard to replicate the Japanese management system and have to settle for a mixture of Japanese and foreign management styles.[8]

There are reasons to regret this. Surely, if you could recruit better staff and operate more along Japanese lines, you would be ahead. But, since this is out of the question, the best solution is to seek an alternative which builds on the strengths of foreign management and avoids the weaknesses of Japanese management. This could be the silver lining in what first looked like a dark cloud.

For starters, if you do recruit high school and college grads fresh from school, as the Japanese do, at least pay more attention to their qualifications than their credentials. The "best" schools do not always turn out the "best" personnel. Graduates of lesser schools may work harder to prove themselves and may have studied harder while in school. You should purposely recruit more staff on the basis of actual skills which they should specialize in rather than a bunch of generalists who have no skills nor wish to acquire them.

A greater emphasis on ability is key. Select competent, trained specialists and let these specialists know that they can rise as quickly as the generalists. Moreover, all of them, specialists and generalists alike, should be promoted more on the basis of what they actually accomplish than on how many years they have been in your employ. Seniority may be an adequate basis for promotion in Japanese firms; in foreign ones, it will simply not work because there are too many mid-career hires. More to the point, if you want a dynamic staff, you must reward ability and initiative.

So much for the broader picture. Certain details may be even more important. As we saw, Japanese factory workers are put to the best possible use, doing the most purposeful tasks as efficiently as possible. You had better be more like the Japanese if you open a factory there. On the other hand, if you run an office, you had better transplant more of your own methods and techniques in order to get a decent day's work out of your white-collar staff. See that they use computers with appropriate software, that they concentrate on specific tasks, and that activity takes precedence over talk. Combined with narrower job descriptions, clearer lines of authority, and greater coordination, these strategies could make your office more efficient than Japanese offices and put you a step ahead.

You could get yet another step ahead by making better use of women, the most wasted of Japan's wasted workers. Even those with ability and ambition are relegated most often to rather menial, second-rate tasks. They also find it harder to be promoted. No wonder so many of them quit young and accomplish rather little while they are around. Foreign companies can certainly make better use of women, giving them more opportunities and rewarding them for their achievements. This is particularly important since it will probably be necessary to employ more women than is done by Japanese companies.

Obviously, you want team players and not just a gang of superstars, so it does not hurt to apply some Japanese practices such as *ringisho, nemawashi*, meetings of all sorts, and a degree of bottom-up decision-making. But do not let it bog down the company. Don't invite as many staff members to meetings, and certainly only those directly concerned, don't take as long to process suggestions or demand as many approvals, and don't take forever to reach a decision. On the other hand, don't forget that the job of managers is to manage so there should be more top-down management than in comparable Japanese firms.

The basic aim should thus be to combine useful Japanese elements, like cooperation, commitment, and loyalty which, in turn, encourage strength and stability, with more dynamic elements like innovation, imagination, and initiative. It is most unlikely that you will ever find exactly the right mix. But it should be possible to field a team that can compete against Japanese rivals.

Probing for Weak Points

Without a doubt, success or failure will be determined to a very large extent by which products (or services) are introduced in the Japanese market. Much of the literature, which shows very little imagination, focuses on the trials and triumphs of manufacturers in Japan and manufacturers are intensely attracted by that market. It may be that these are the more epic struggles or that, as *macho* businessmen put it, "if you can make it in Japan, you can make it anywhere."

While something can be said for that approach, it is certainly less rational than to do what has been suggested all along, namely take on the Japanese where they are weakest and not where they are strongest. Manufacturing, as we shall see later, should not be ruled out. But there are many other areas where the chances of success are considerably greater.

As everyone knows, Japan's farmers are dreadfully unproductive, not because they are lazy but because the farms are too small and labor too costly. This is not likely to change dramatically for some time to come. Agricultural produce remains an extremely promising line. The only problem is that there are still some artificial barriers. As these come down, it will be feasible to sell more and more to Japan.

But it is already possible to enter the market with processed foods, which are protected to a lesser extent and which, by the way, offer more added value. This can apply to quite ordinary items, like cheese, canned goods, even dog food. Others sell well because of a special cachet among consumers such as French wines, Swiss chocolates, German sausages and so on. There are still plenty of these articles which have yet to be introduced in Japan and could be tried, many produced by smaller companies.

Processed natural resources are of the same nature. In this case, the problem is partly artificial barriers. Raw materials do get in easier than processed ones. The real edge for foreigners is that processing raw materials in Japan is so expensive. The biggest cost for many is electricity, generated by expensive coal or oil which also has to be imported and which, in addition, may be more polluting than the Japanese now permit. There is also the question of space, lacking in that tight country, which is often needed for processing. Resource producers should keep pushing for increased processing before export. They may find that they are pushing on an open door.

Less noticed, but considerably more promising, are any number of services. In this sector, as already explained, the Japanese are grossly inefficient whenever they equate service with a heavy use of high quality personnel. If you are dealing in more exclusive, upmarket areas, it may not be possible to evade this cost any more than the Japanese. The only advantage a foreign company would have is, again, an aura of foreignness. Nonetheless, this can make a difference for sports clubs, language schools, or fancy restaurants.

But greater opportunities exist where foreign companies know how to use personnel better and have more accomplished by fewer. Here, U.S. companies have an excellent track record, especially for fast foods. Not only are they considerably more efficient, they manage to maintain an admirable level of service tinged with some foreign glamour. A "Big Mac" may look banal to you, but to a Japanese teenager it can be a culinary adventure. The same applies to fried chicken, donuts, and bagels. And, in some retailing branches, Western companies had a notable headstart, as with convenience stores, specialty shops, do-it-yourself corners, and fashion boutiques. Here, too, foreign players are often more efficient or, if nothing else, exotic.

Fast food and retailing are just the more obvious entry points. The tertiary sector is vast, well over half the total economy, and there is an incredible number of other areas where foreign firms are ahead of the Japanese. This includes some forms of insurance, consumer finance, leasing, public relations, health care, etc. One good example is fund management, where foreign brokers use more rational methods in picking stocks and achieved better performance than Japanese competitors.

Quite naturally, manufacturing is a much tougher sector for foreigners to crack, but there are definite possibilities. It must be remembered that the Japanese are not tops for everything. Indeed, since they specialize heavily and target favored areas, they must neglect others and it is worthwhile seeking them out. The upmarket ones are more obvious, like telecommunications and aerospace. Many more can be found at lower levels, including such items as furniture and house furnishings, larger household appliances and even prefabricated houses. More surprising is that consumer electronics can again be sold in Japan, namely less sophisticated ones like radios, tape recorders, and even VCRs.

In short, like every other country, Japan does not have a comparative advantage everywhere. Once it was competitive for cheap, labor-intensive goods. But this edge possibly no longer exists, which explains why neighboring Asian countries can sell not only cheaper electronics, but garments, textiles, toys, watches, and lots of other products. Despite strenuous efforts, it still has not reached the top of the range for some goods, which leaves room for fancy Swiss watches, German shavers, Danish audio equipment, and Germany luxury cars.

In this whole discussion, we have not used a word which appears too frequently elsewhere, namely "unique." There is a widespread notion that only "unique" products (or services) can succeed on the Japanese market. This is nonsense! First of all, there are simply not that many unique articles around. Secondly, most would not remain unique for long, given the Japanese ability to imitate. Thirdly, and most significant, a look at which products have succeeded will show that terribly few are unique, but nearly all are somehow superior. They are easier to use, better designed, more durable, of finer quality or, not to be forgotten, simply cheaper. Their products have succeeded on comparative advantage as opposed to some absolute difference.

This sort of advantage is extremely important for there are huge numbers of products which do enjoy a comparative advantage. There are some products which are still more technologically advanced or offer better quality. There are ever more which are considerably cheaper. Indeed, for the first time in recent history, being cheaper has become the crucial selling point of many imported articles. This is a wonderful opening for less developed countries which until now did not stand a chance.

When selecting the product (or service), it is also very useful to consider yet another weakness. As noted, in Japan's dual structure, there is a small number of very large companies and a large number of pretty small ones. It may happen that your competitors figure among the larger, more powerful ones. In this case, it might be wiser to try another product. On the other hand, the chief rivals may be rather small companies, small compared not only to foreign multinationals but quite ordinary foreign firms. Here the competition will be much easier to beat.

There are so many examples of this that only a sampling is necessary. Foreign food processing and beverage companies are much larger than Japan's biggest (two to six times the size), and the same applies to chemical and pharmaceutical producers (two to five times) and paper and pulp manufacturers (twice as big) and nonferrous metals. Even for computers, semiconductors, and electrical equipment, U.S. and European giants could readily take on medium-sized Japanese firms.[9] For aerospace and defense equipment, even large Japanese producers are fairly small.

Obviously, in deciding which products or services have a comparative advantage and which companies have a competitive edge, it is necessary to go beyond generalities and undertake detailed market and competition studies. This is often forgotten by companies which simply assume that Japan is a tough market. If you choose well, it may not be anywhere near as tough as it seemed.

Wising Up

Over the years, many ideas have been floated about how to compete against the Japanese and many strategies have been tried. Some have worked, some have not. To be perfectly frank, more have not worked than have. Still, there does seem to be a tendency for things to go less poorly for Japan's competitors now that foreign companies have had more experience and are gradually wising up. The following examples are just a small sampling of what has been done. There is much, much more.

For starters, it is increasingly evident to all that it is essential to take on the Japanese in Japan. This has been stated by many business leaders, one of the more illuminating comments coming from Ned C. Lautenbach, head of IBM's operations in Asia. "Our most important competitors are in Japan, and we have to fight them on their territory. They implement their technology first here, and it's important to compete against it first here. We can't just wait for them to come to the U.S."[10]

This sort of comment is not surprising for a company that has always been in the forefront. But, it is now joined by Apple Computers, which waited far too long, most of the semi-conductor makers and, better late than never, many of the automakers. It is a pity they did not realize this earlier. Not only are these companies present, they are offering some of their best products, in several cases, even before they are available at home, such as IBM's notebook computer and Apple's handwriting recognition system. Procter & Gamble came out with special diapers for Japanese babies' bottoms and Coca Cola sells certain soft drinks only in Japan.

As for price, it has finally dawned on foreigners that low prices can be a selling point. Apple, which muffed its original entry, realized that price matters and cut average prices in half. Most other foreign companies have not gone as far but they have decided that, to gain market share, lower prices over a longer time is the best policy. Meanwhile, the surrounding, newly industrialized countries are flooding Japan with all sorts of goods, some unloaded cheaper than you could get them from even the cheapest Japanese maker, and special NIC stores were opened.

Once upon a time, most foreign companies went into joint ventures, even when not obligatory. Now, more and more are going it alone and some have dissolved earlier partnerships to gain greater control. Even those which opt for joint ventures are less naive. LSI Logic went into a first arrangement with rival Toshiba, which soon learned its techniques. The second time around, it cooperated with outsider Kawasaki Steel, which will find it harder to copy. Just in case, LSI insisted on a 55 percent share, which gives it more control.[11]

The key to Japan's market is distribution. Even if they were not satisfied with their distributors, foreign companies just lumped it in past years. Now, they are setting up their own distribution networks. This has been most noticeable for pharmaceutical companies and automakers, with BMW leading the way. Other companies have successfully pioneered direct sales, including Amway and Tupperware. Coca Cola stuck to local distributors, but *it* pulls the strings.

Once the biggest news was about investments by major manufacturers. Then came the bankers and brokers. Well, the latest dope is that they all earned a small share of the market, but few got much further. However, since foreign companies have entered services and distribution, the results appear much more heartening. In fact, McDonald's, Colonel Sanders, Pizza Hut, and their ilk dominate the fast foods sector. Foreign chains like Seven-Eleven nearly created the convenience store boom and Aux Printemps opened one of the ritziest department stores. But that is not all, Toys 'R' Us and Blockbuster Video now plan to operate stores nationwide, bigger and better stores than any of their rivals. Since many of these rivals are mom-and-pop ventures or small chains, they should succeed.

Meanwhile, with regard to some aspects of Japanese management, foreigners now openly admit their past folly. They were wrong to overlook quality, they were wrong to forget productivity, they were even wrong to mistreat ordinary workers (although that last comment is heard less often). And they are trying to make amends. Throughout the U.S., Europe, and Asia, quality control circles are emerging, suggestion boxes are being installed, and jolly productivity campaigns are launched. This is a step in the right direction, although it will take many more to catch up.

Some companies have gone even further in their "learn from Japan" attempts. One is Harley-Davidson, which has particularly ugly memories of mistakes it should not have committed. To spur a turnaround, it introduced three quality tenets which became known as the "Harley productivity triad." They were just-in-time inventory, making everybody in the plant responsible for quality ("employee involvement" it was called), and having workers check whether they met specifications.[12] Sound familiar?

But nobody went further than NUMMI, New United Motor Manufacturing Incorporated. GM, finally shamed into admitting it was beat, cooperated with Toyota, one of those that beat it. Together, they worked out the closest thing to Japanese-style management abroad. This included quality control, productivity enhancement, job enlargement, job rotation, and teamwork under a team leader. There was to be more job security, better relations between workers and supervisors, and some bottom-up decision-making. In addition, equipment was upgraded. NUMMI did not quite live up to its expectations. But it did teach American managers and workers some useful lessons.

One of the few things Western workers really liked about the Japanese system was job security, mostly because their economies were slowing down and more employees were worried about being laid off. But they did not realize that Japan's own "lifetime" employment had emerged at a time when workers were needed urgently by expanding companies. So, although they made some progress, they did not get very far. Still, to some extent, there was convergence as job security was emphasized in the West and reduced in Japan.

Last but certainly not least, despite the cost and difficulties of operating in Japan, foreign companies were earning bigger profits there than comparable Japanese companies. This was reported regularly over an extended period by the Ministry of International Trade and Industry, the American Chamber of Commerce in Japan, and the European Business Community.[13] Considering that foreign managers were in it for profits more than market share, yet had to compete with Japanese rivals which did everything possible to squeeze their margins, this is quite an achievement.

As stated, the purpose of this section is just to show that things are happening, that companies are learning, that there is hope. If more were learned, and more were to happen, then perhaps Japan might face real competition in the years to come and more foreigners could beat the Japanese at their own game. ∎

Notes

1. James B. Shuman, "Easy Rider Rides Again," *Business Tokyo*, July 1991, p. 27.

2. The best example is the U.S. television industry, subjected to massive dumping and collusion by Japanese producers, which expired before relief came. See Marvin J. Wolf, *The Japanese Conspiracy*.

3. See Woronoff, *Japanese Targeting*.

4. John E. Rehfeld, "What Working for a Japanese Company Taught Me," *Harvard Business Review*, November-December 1990, p. 174. It may be just as well to read the whole article by the CEO of Seiko Instruments USA and former general manager of Toshiba America's computer business.

5. For more information on how to penetrate the Japanese market, see the books listed under "Doing Business in Japan," in the bibliography.

6. On pros and cons of using joint ventures, see P. Reed Maurer, *Competing in Japan*, and Mark Zimmerman, *How To Do Business With The Japanese*.

7. Czinkota and Woronoff, op. cit., pp. 68-70.

8. For more on recruitment and use of Japanese personnel, see Woronoff, *The No-Nonsense Guide To Doing Business in Japan,* pp. 95-107.

9. Dodwell, *Industrial Groupings in Japan,* pp. 24-30.

10. *Wall Street Journal,* July 17, 1991, p. 10.

11. *Business Week,* p. 97.

12. *Business Tokyo,* July 1991, pp. 28-29.

13. See Tomoko Hamada, *American Enterprise in Japan,* pp. 33-35.

Glossary

amae - dependence

arubaito - part-time job

bucho - department head

chusei-shin - loyalty

endaka - heavy yen

furita - "freeter," freelancer

gambare - persevere, endure

haken-shain - temp

hanko - seal

ippan shoku - general work, slow track

kacho - section head

kacho-byo - *kacho*'s disease

kaigi - formal conference

kaizen - continuous improvement

kanban-hoshiki - just-in-time inventory system

karoshi - death from overwork

kato kyoso - excessive competition

keiretsu - group

kessai - approval

kitanai, kiken, kitsui - dirty, dangerous, demanding

kobun - follower

kondankai - informal meeting

madogiwa zoku - "window-sill tribe"

moretsu shain - dynamic employee

nemawashi - informal consultation

nenko joretsu - promotion by seniority

nihonteki keiei - Japanese-style management

ningen kankei - human relations

ringisho - proposal

samurai - warrior

sarariman - "salaryman," salaried employee

sempai - senior

shinjinrui - new human race

shirake sedai - reactionless generation

sogo shoku - comprehensive work, fast track

shushinkoyo - *lifetime employment*

tenshoku - changing jobs

wa - harmony

zaibatsu - prewar trusts

zaiteku - "financial technology"

zenrei - precedent

Bibliography

1. Japanese-Style Management

Aoki, Masahiko, *Information, Incentives, and Bargaining in the Japanese Economy*, Cambridge, Cambridge University Press, 1988.

Arai, Shunzo, *An Intersection of East and West, Japanese Business Management*, Tokyo, Rikugei, 1971.

Hayashi, Shuji, *Culture and Management in Japan*, Tokyo, University of Tokyo Press, 1989.

Kono, Toyohiro, *Strategy & Structure of Japanese Enterprises*, London, Macmillan, 1984.

Lincoln, James R., and Arne L. Kalleberg, *Culture, Control and Commitment*, Cambridge, Cambridge University Press, 1990.

Lu, David J., *Inside Corporate Japan, The Art of Fumble-Free Management*, Cambridge, Productivity Press, 1982.

Makino, Noboru, *Decline and Prosperity, Corporate Innovation in Japan*, Tokyo, Kodansha, 1987.

Odaka, Kunio, *Japanese Management—A Forward-Looking Analysis*, Tokyo, Asian Productivity Organization, 1986.

Ouchi, William, *Theory Z*, Reading, Addison-Wesley, 1981.

Pascale, Richard Tanner, and Anthony G. Athos, *The Art of Japanese Management*, New York, Simon and Shuster, 1981.

Sasaki, Naoto, *Management & Industrial Structure in Japan*, Oxford, Pergamon Press, 1981.

Sato, Kazuo, and Yasuo Hoshino, *The Anatomy of Japanese Business*, Armonk, M.E. Sharpe, 1984.

Sethi, S. Prakash, Nobuaki Namiki, and Carl L. Swanson, *The False Promise of the Japanese Miracle*, Boston, Pitman, 1984.

Shimabukuro, Yoshiaki, *Consensus Management in Japanese Industry*, Tokyo, I.S.S., 1982.

Yoshino, M.Y., *Japan's Managerial System*, Cambridge, MIT Press, 1968.

2. Industrial Relations

Abegglen, James C., *The Japanese Factory*, Glenco, Free Press, 1958.

Chalmers, Norma J., *Industrial Relations in Japan, The Peripheral Workforce*, London, Routledge, 1989.

Cole, Robert E., *Japanese Blue Collar: The Changing Tradition*, Berkeley, University of California Press, 1971.

_____, *Work, Mobility, and Participation*, Berkeley, University of California Press, 1979.

Dore, Ronald P., *British Factory, Japanese Factory*, Berkeley, University of California Press, 1973.

Hanami, Tadashi, *Labor Relations in Japan Today*, Tokyo, Kodansha International, 1979.

Inohara, Hideo, *Human Resource Development in Japanese Companies*, Tokyo, Asian Productivity Organization, 1990.

Kamata, Satoshi, *Japan In The Passing Lane*, New York, Pantheon, 1982.

Kinzley, W. Dean, *Industrial Harmony in Modern Japan, The Invention of a Tradition*, London, Routledge, 1991.

Koike, Kazuo, *Understanding Industrial Relations in Modern Japan*, New York, St. Martin's Press, 1988.

Levine, Solomon B., and Hisashi Kawada, *Human Resources in Japanese Industrial Development*, Princeton, Princeton University Press, 1991.

Marsh, Robert M. and Hiroshi Mannari, *Modernization and the Japanese Factory*, Princeton, Princeton University Press, 1976.

Shirao, Taishiro ed., *Contemporary Industrial Relations in Japan*, Madison, University of Wisconsin Press, 1983.

Sumiya, Mikio, *The Japanese Industrial Relations Reconsidered*, Tokyo, Japan Institute of Labor, 1990.

Taira, Koji, *Economic Development and the Labor Market in Japan*, New York, Columbia University Press, 1970.

Whitehall, Arthur M., and Shin-Ichi Takezawa, *The Other Worker*, Honolulu, East-West Center Press, 1968.

3. The Japanese Company

Abegglen, James C., and George Stalk, Jr., *Kaisha, The Japanese Corporation*, New York, Basic Books, 1985.

Abegglen, James C., *The Strategy of Japanese Business*, Cambridge, Ballinger, 1984.

Ballon, Robert J., and Iwao Tomita, *The Financial Behavior of Japanese Corporations*, Tokyo, Kodansha International, 1988.

Clark, Rodney, *The Japanese Company*, New Haven, Yale University Press, 1979.

Dodwell Marketing Consultants, *Industrial Groupings in Japan*, Tokyo, annual.

Kester, W. Carl, *Japanese Takeovers*, Boston, Harvard Business School Press, 1990.

Kondo, Dorinne K., *Crafting Selves: Power, Gender and Discourses of Identity in a Japanese Workplace*, Chicago, University of Chicago Press, 1989.

Rohlen, Thomas P., *For Harmony and Strength*, Berkeley, University of California Press, 1974.

Small and Medium Enterprise Agency, *White Paper on Small and Medium Enterprises in Japan*, Tokyo, annual.

Smitka, Michael J., *Competitive Ties, Subcontracting in the Japanese Automotive Industry*, Princeton, Princeton University Press, 1991.

4.   Quality Control, Productivity, Etc.

Imai, Masaaki, *Kaizen, The Key to Japan's Competitive Success*, New York, McGraw Hill, 1986.

Ishikawa, Kaoru, *What Is Total Quality Control? The Japanese Way*, Englewood Cliffs, Prentice Hall, 1985.

Japan Productivity Center, *Strategies for Productivity, International Perspectives*, Tokyo, UNIPUB, 1984.

Schodt, Frederik L., *Inside the Robot Kingdom*, Tokyo, Kodansha, 1990.

Walton, Mary, *The Deming Management Method*, New York, Perigree, 1986.

Womack, James P., Daniel T. Jones, and Daniel Roos, *The Machine That Changed The World*, New York, Macmillan, 1990.

5.   Japanese Companies, Founders

Alletzhauser, Albert J., *The House of Nomura*, New York, Harper, 1990.

Fruin, W. Mark, *Kikkoman, Company, Clan, and Community*, Cambridge, Harvard University Press, 1983.

Kobayashi, Koji, *Rising To The Challenge*, Tokyo, Harcourt Brace Jovanovich Japan, 1989.

Matsushita, Konosuke, *Not For Bread Alone, A Business Ethos, A Management Ethic*, Kyoto, PHP Institute, 1984.

_____ , *Quest For Prosperity*, Kyoto, PHP Institute, 1988.

Morita, Akio, *Made In Japan, Akio Morita and Sony*, New York, E.P. Dutton, 1986.

Toyoda, Eiji, *Toyota, Fifty Years in Motion*, Tokyo, Kodansha, 1985.

Toyota Motor Corp., *Toyota, A History of the First 50 Years*, Tokyo, Toyota Motor Corp., 1988.

6.   Women Workers

Cook, Alice, and Hiroko Hayashi, *Working Women in Japan: Discrimination, Resistance, and Reform*, Ithaca, Cornell University Press, 1980.

Lo, Jeannie, *Office Ladies, Factory Women*, Armonk, M.E. Sharpe, 1990.

Ministry of Labor, *White Paper on Women's Labor*, annual.

Saso, Mary, *Women in the Japanese Workplace*, London, Hilary Shipman, 1990.

7. Japanese Management Abroad

Edgington, David W., *Japanese Business Down Under, Patterns of Japanese Investment in Australia*, London, Routledge, 1990.

Fucini, Joseph J. and Suzy Fucini, *Working for the Japanese: Inside Mazda's American Auto Plant*, New York, Free Press, 1990.

Gelsanliter, David, *Jump Start: Japan Comes to the Heartland*, Farrar, Straus, Giroux, 1990.

Fukuda, K. John, *Japanese-Style Management Transferred, The Experience of East Asia*, London, Routledge, 1988.

Shibagaki, Kazuo, Malcolm Trevor, and Tetsuo Abe, *Japanese And European Management, Their International Adaptability*, Tokyo, University of Tokyo Press, 1989.

Woronoff, Jon, *Japan's Commercial Empire*, Armonk, M.E. Sharpe, and London, Macmillan, 1984.

Yamashita, Shoichi, *Transfer of Japanese Technology and Management to the Asean Countries*, Tokyo, University of Tokyo Press, 1990.

8. Doing Business With Japan

Czinkota, Michael, and Jon Woronoff, *Unlocking Japan's Markets: Seizing Marketing and Distribution Opportunities in Today's Japan*, Chicago, Probus Publishing, 1991.

Hamada, Tomoko, *American Enterprise in Japan*, Albany, SUNY Press, 1991.

Huddleston, Jr., Jackson N., *Gaijin Kaisha, Running A Foreign Business in Japan*, Armonk, M.E. Sharpe, 1990.

Kang, T.W., *Gaishi, The Foreign Company in Japan*, New York, Basic Books, 1990.

Maurer, P. Reed, *Competing in Japan*, Tokyo, Japan Times, 1989.

Morgan, James C., and Jeffrey J. Morgan, *Cracking The Japanese Market*, New York, Free Press, 1991.

Woronoff, Jon, *The "No-Nonsense" Guide to Doing Business in Japan,* Tokyo, Yohan, 1991.

Zimmerman, Mark, *How To Do Business With The Japanese, A Strategy For Success,* New York, Random House, 1985.

9. Economic, Social, and Political Background

Cusumano, Michael A., *Japan's Software Factories,* Oxford, Oxford University Press, 1991.

Doi, Takeo, *The Anatomy of Dependence,* Tokyo, Kodansha International, 1973.

Duke, Benjamin, *The Japanese School, Lessons for Industrial America,* New York, Praeger Press, 1986.

Economic Planning Agency, *White Paper on National Life,* Tokyo, annual.

Emmott, Bill, *The Sun Also Sets,* New York, Random House, 1988.

Gibney, Frank, *Miracle by Design, The Real Reasons Behind Japan's Economic Success,* New York, Times Books, 1982.

Levine, Solomon B., and Koji Taira, *Japan's External Economic Relations: Japanese Perspectives,* Newbury Park, Sage Publications, 1991.

Ministry of Labor, *Survey of Japanese Employees' Life After Retirement,* Tokyo, annual.

_____ , *White Paper on Labor,* Tokyo, annual.

Romberg, Alan D., and Tadashi Yamamoto eds., *Same Bed, Different Dreams,* New York, Council on Foreign Relations Press, 1990.

Van Der Meer, Cornelius L.J., and Saburo Yamada, *Japanese Agriculture,* London, Routledge, 1990.

Vogel, Ezra F., *Japan As Number One, Lessons For America,* Cambridge, Cambridge University Press, 1988.

_____ , ed., *Modern Japanese Organization and Decision-Making*, Berkeley, University of California Press, 1975.

Wolf, Marvin J., *The Japanese Conspiracy*, New York, Empire Books, 1983.

Woronoff, Jon, *Japan As—Anything But—Number One*, London, Macmillan, and Armonk, M.E. Sharpe, 1991.

_____ , *Japanese Targeting, Successes, Failures, Lessons*, London, Macmillan, and New York, St. Martin's Press, 1992.

_____ , *Japan: The (Coming) Economic Crisis*, Tokyo, Yohan, 1992.

_____ , *Politics, The Japanese Way*, London, Macmillan, and New York, St. Martin's Press, 1988.

Index

A

Abegglen, James, 12-3, 138, 158
administrative reform, 132-3
aging, 123
agriculture, 32, 108-14, 201
Akihabara, 117
amae, 83-4
American Chamber of Commerce in Japan, 208
Amway, 206
Apple Computers, 205
Arai, Shunzo, 146

D

E

F

U

United States, 4, 15, 25, 30-1, 33-5, 39-40, 71, 102, 109, 111-4, 118-9, 120, 131, 205
Uno, Sousuke, 132

V

Victor Company of Japan (JVC), 153, 159-60
Vogel, Ezra, 78, 145

W

wages, 39, 52, 79, 87, 92-3, 116, 167, 192
weaknesses, 3-5, 7, 9-12, 24, 27-8, 37-40, 50-3, 56-7, 137-61
welfare, 61-2, 90-1, 131
women, 32, 45, 69-73, 168, 170, 176, 181, 193, 200
workers,
  blue-collar, 22-30, 32, 43-4, 59, 65, 173, 179;
  foreign, 171-7, 179-81;
  white-collar, 32, 43-73
work will, 81-90
Woronoff's laws, 148-9

Y

Yamaha, 138, 158
YKK, 37

Z

zaibatsu, 68, 103
zaiteku, 154-5

About the Publisher

PROBUS PUBLISHING COMPANY

Probus Publishing Company fills the informational needs of today's business professional by publishing authoritative, quality books on timely and relevant topics, including:

- Investing
- Futures/Options Trading
- Banking
- Finance
- Marketing and Sales
- Manufacturing and Project Management
- Personal Finance, Real Estate, Insurance and Estate Planning
- Entrepreneurship
- Management

Probus books are available at quantity discounts when purchased for business, educational or sales promotional use. For more information, please call the Director, Corporate/Institutional Sales at 1-800-PROBUS-1, or write:

Director, Corporate/Institutional Sales
Probus Publishing Company
1925 N. Clybourn Avenue
Chicago, Illinois 60614
FAX (312) 868-6250